900
Rt

DR. JOYCE
BROTHERS

THE SUCCESSFUL WOMAN

*HOW YOU CAN HAVE A CAREER,
A HUSBAND AND A FAMILY—
AND NOT FEEL GUILTY ABOUT IT*

SIMON AND SCHUSTER

New York   London   Toronto   Sydney   Tokyo

Copyright © 1988 by Joyce B. Enterprises, Inc.
All rights reserved
including the right of reproduction
in whole or in part in any form
Published by Simon and Schuster
A Division of Simon & Schuster Inc.
Simon & Schuster Building
Rockefeller Center
1230 Avenue of the Americas
New York, NY 10020

SIMON AND SCHUSTER and colophon are registered trademarks
of Simon & Schuster Inc.

Designed by Irving Perkins Associates
Manufactured in the United States of America

10 9 8 7 6 5 4 3 2 1

Library of Congress Cataloging in Publication Data
Brothers, Joyce.

The successful woman : how you can have a career, a husband,
and a family— and not feel guilty about it / Joyce Brothers.
p.   cm.
Includes index.
1. Dual-career families—United States.   2. Work and family—
United States.   3. Women in the professions—United States.
4. Women executives—United States.   5. Success in business—United
States.   I. Title.
HQ536.B766 1988
306.8'7—dc19   *88-3082*
ISBN 0-671-55265-1   *CIP*

CONTENTS

ACKNOWLEDGMENTS

I WANT to thank the women who allowed me and my researchers to interview them for their generous sharing of their experiences, their insights, their problems.

I particularly want to thank Lisa Arbisser, Estelle Bauer, Helen Gurley Brown, Joyce Buchman, Julia Child, Pat Collins, Heloise Cruse, Mary Cunningham, Julie Nixon Eisenhower, Karol Emmerich, Joni Evans, Nancy Evans, Sybil Ferguson, Lynn Gilbert, Linda Grant, Phyllis Harrison-Ross, M.D., Claire Heiss, Barbara Hendricks, Jun Kanai, Jane Kennedy, Jacqueline Leo, Ambassador Jeane Kirkpatrick, Sheila Kurtz, Sherry Lansing, Lana Jane Lewis-Brent, Marilyn Moore, Karen Nussbaum, Ponchitta Pierce, Sally Quinn, Lynn Redgrave, Joan Rivers, Ida Roberts, Felice Schwartz, Carole Sinclair, Gillian Martin Sorensen, Linda Tarry, Chris Boe Voran, Barbara Walters, Terry Weill, M.D., Lois Wyse and those successful women who requested anonymity.

I do not want readers to assume, however, that I or my researchers interviewed every woman who is quoted in this book. Some women who are quoted very briefly, including Prime Minister Margaret Thatcher, Mrs. Ronald Reagan, Nobel Prize–winner Professor Rita Levi-Montalcini and others, were not interviewed. These brief quotes were picked up from interviews with these women published in newspapers and magazines and from speeches they had given that were published in whole or in part in the press.

I am deeply grateful to Susan Howard Biederman, who was my wonderful and sensitive right hand as an interviewer; Susan Lehman, who worked hard, long and cheerfully, transcribing the taped interviews, and Thelma Kandell.

PART ONE

THE HAPPIEST WOMAN OF ALL

ONE

The great question that has never been answered, and which I have not yet been able to answer, despite my thirty years of research into the feminine soul, is "What does a woman want?"

SIGMUND FREUD asked his famous question several generations of women ago. He would not need to ask today. We all know the answer.

A woman wants everything a man wants. Success and power and status and money. Love and marriage and children. Happiness. Fulfillment. And for the first time in history, the doors are open for women to go out and get what they want. Many women have opted to "have it all"—career, marriage, children. And they have gone out, primed with idealism and ambition, to get it all.

But something happened on the way to success.

And something happened to marriage.

And something happened to motherhood.

It reminds me of the time Milt and I gave Lisa a Polaroid camera for her ninth birthday. After her father explained how to use the camera, Lisa lined up all the birthday-party guests for her first photograph. She peered through the viewfinder for long seconds and finally pushed the button. After the prescribed time, she proudly drew out the picture. As she looked at it, her face fell. It was blurred.

"Everybody moved!" she exclaimed.

In the world of women today, everybody *has* moved. Life is not the way it used to be. Nor is it the way women were led to believe it would be.

Women were sold a bill of goods. They were told that they could—and should—have it all. A successful career, a good husband, a wonderful marriage, great children. If they had anything less, it was because they were lazy or weak, lacked ambition or self-esteem, were inadequate human beings.

This is nonsense, of course. No one can have it all. Men do not—and cannot. Neither can women. But women can have *almost* all of it. They can have what they want most. They can have more than men will ever have.

In this book I am going to tell you how women like television's Barbara Walters and Joan Rivers, Ambassador Jeane Kirkpatrick, author Julie Nixon Eisenhower, Diet Center founder Sybil Ferguson, master cook Julia Child, film producer Sherry Lansing, actress Lynn Redgrave and dozens of other successful women in business, the professions, the arts, politics and government balance career and family to get what they want most out of life.

These are real women who have faced real problems. They are privileged women who have more money and more status than the average woman—and they have earned that money and that status. Nevertheless, they face the same problems as every other working woman. Their coping mechanisms can work as well for you as they do for them.

Two

In the 1950s when I embarked on my career as a media psychologist, I had a daily radio program on WNBC in New York City on which people called in for advice on their problems.

The great majority of women callers had marriage problems. Their husbands were unfaithful. Or alcoholic. Or brutal. They were angry or hurtfully critical. Stingy, domineering, cold. "What can I do?" women asked me. "How can I cope?"

The common denominator was fear—fear of their marriages disintegrating. Most married women in the 1950s were housewives. If they had worked before marriage, it had usually been at low-level, low-status jobs. They were not equipped to support themselves and their children. They were trapped. If a woman left her husband, her lot would be even worse.

As I contrast those women of the 1950s with the women who write to me with their problems today, I realize just how great the revolution in women's lives has been. In the 1950s, it was clear that women's major problem was the marriage.

But the letters I get now tend to be about their problems in combining work and family life.

Women are well equipped to deal with the business and professional world today. It is their marriages that are tearing them apart. Most of the old rules that shaped their parents' marriages no longer apply, and very few new rules have been formulated.

They write about husbands who do not pull their weight around the house, expecting their wives to do the shopping, cleaning and cooking on top of their full-time jobs—jobs that are often on a par with or superior to their husbands' jobs in terms of both status and salary.

They write about husbands who sulk when their wives have to attend a business convention and husbands who refuse to accompany their wives to business dinners.

They ask what to do when they bring home a briefcase full of research that must be whipped into shape to present at tomorrow morning's nine o'clock meeting—and their husband makes it clear he wants to spend the evening making love.

They write, "My lover insists we get married. He wants children. But I don't know. My life is full now. Do I want to be a wife? A mother? Will I lose him if I say I like things the way they are now?"

They want to know how to handle it when they discover their husbands are jealous of their boss—without reason.

They write about husbands who become impotent when their wives start earning more money than they do.

They tell me that their two-year-old has nightmares and their four-year-old cries when they drop her off at nursery school and their husbands blame them and say they are warping their children's lives by insisting on working instead of staying home, but their husbands share no part of caring for the children.

They complain that their husbands try to sabotage their careers.

They write that they keep thinking about divorce. "I need a little peace in my life."

There is anger—a lot of anger—in these letters. And sadness. Bewilderment. Frustration. Exasperation. A longing for reassurance. And guilt. So much guilt.

Matina Horner, psychologist and president of Radcliffe, whose research two decades ago revealed that fear of success was blocking many women from achieving their career goals, now reports that women have conquered that fear. Today they fear they will not be able to integrate career and marriage, that one or the other will suffer from neglect. Today's women want success, but more and more are saying they do not want it if the price is sacrificing marriage and children.

A survey of the Radcliffe class of 1985 one year after graduation reinforces this. Ninety percent of the graduates reported that they were either working or actively looking for work. Ninety-one percent of the graduates wanted to have at least one child. Ninety-seven percent of the single women said they hoped to marry. And married or single, their great concern was that they would not be able to handle both marriage and a career. They were aware that women only ten and fifteen years older were complaining of burnout and resigning from prestigious jobs. A law student at Columbia University told me about her older sister. "Marnie spent eight years on the up escalator after she got her MBA. She was vice president for production in a Fortune 1000 company and earning more than fifty thousand dollars a year. And one day she quit. Cold! She said she couldn't take it any longer. Now she stays home and takes care of her two kids, and all she talks about is her soaps and what to have for dinner.

"When I think about her, I wonder. Do I really want to be a lawyer? Perhaps I'd rather just be a wife and mother? Except I've always dreamed of arguing a case before the Supreme Court. But I do want to get married and have kids.

On the other hand, the life my sister has now would drive me crazy." She sighed. "I wish I knew what the right choice is."

What I want to tell women in this book is that there is no need for the pendulum to swing back to the 1950s. Women *can* have a career and marriage and children—and a wonderful life.

I urge you to choose whatever it is you want most in life and go after it. You don't have to choose marriage and career and children. Choose two. Or one. Choose what you want. It is your life. If you decide you want all three, go for it. But go for it with your eyes wide open and a realistic level of expectation.

"Ten years ago I would have been appalled at the life I am leading," novelist Sara Davidson confessed. "All my time is spent on three things: baby, work, and keeping the marriage going. Sometimes I feel I'm dying inside this life. Gone are an active social life, travel, hobbies, recreational activities.

"I find I can handle two beautifully. When my husband is out of town, or when I'm between projects and not working, things go smoothly. But three pushes me to the edge. Someone is unhappy, something is always getting short shrift."

Don't fool yourself that you are going to have it all. You are not. Psychologically, having it all is not even a valid concept. The marvelous thing about human beings is that we are perpetually reaching for the stars. The more we have, the more we want. And for this reason, we never have it all.

Five years, ten years from now, you may reach the goals that you set for yourself today, goals that you think of as having it all. You will discover that they are no longer enough. You will aspire to more. As Dolly Parton put it, "When they say less is more, I say 'That's a crock!' *More* is more, and I want more. I've always wanted more."

One hears of superwomen who have it all, but I have never met one. "I don't know what the 'having it all' statement means," says actress Lynn Redgrave. "It somehow implies that everything will be perfect. And nothing is. I don't think anybody's life is without some compromise, without ups and downs. And without the downs, how could one possibly enjoy the ups?"

"Nobody has it all," says Gillian Sorensen, New York City Commissioner for the United Nations and Consular Corps. "If you want five children, you cannot have a full-time job. If you want to earn half a million dollars a year, you cannot have children and a thriving marriage. At least, I don't think so. Something has to give. If you want to work fourteen hours a day, you can't spend time on your home. It's always an adjustment. The adjustments are different things at different times.

"No man has it all either. If he concentrates on his career, something in his family life gives. The difficult thing is to strike the balance that makes you a challenged, active and fulfilled person."

Mary Cunningham, president of Semper Enterprises, a venture-capital and strategic-consulting firm formed in partnership with her husband, William Agee, says, "The complaint that we as women had twenty-five or fifty years ago was basically that the perimeters of our lives were so narrowly defined that we did not have any choices. We very justifiably complained about our lack of control over our lives.

"So today I find it disturbing that with many more choices, we are starting to hear complaints about having too many choices and not knowing how to balance all the options. We are in an inherently better position than we were half a century ago, when the complaint was: Can I have just one more thing?

"That is the backdrop in my mind when people ask, 'Can you have a marriage, be a mother and have a successful career all at once?' The answer is yes, depending on how you choose to do it. You have to choose the right marriage. You have to raise the right child—by which I mean raise the right expectations in that child. And you have to choose the right career.

"I could put three things together that would be contradictory, in conflict all the time, and I would be beating my head against the wall and never be in balance. I could choose a man who would resent every moment I spent on my job. I could raise a child who would be real trouble if I were gone for six hours a day.

"What it amounts to is that if you want those three things, you must make choices that give you a fighting chance of having them all."

"I think you can *do* it all if you really want to," says Pat Collins, former arts and entertainment editor on the *CBS Morning News*, who now heads her own company which develops shows for television syndication. "You can have your babies, be married and work outside the home. *Having* it all is a much fuzzier concept. I don't know anyone who has it all. I know women with beautiful homes and successful husbands and great careers and perfect children with perfect orthodonture who are miserable, and I know women whose husbands and homes and kids and jobs are not all of the above and who are very happy and at peace with themselves.

"I'm not persuaded that there is such a thing as *having* it all. What's that wonderful John Lennon quote? Something like life is what happens while you're busy planning everything else. I think that is the absolute truth."

Karol Emmerich, vice president and treasurer of Dayton-Hudson in Minneapolis, says, "Most people I went to high school with would probably say that I have it all. But it is physically impossible. My idea of having it all is being able to do everything—not just what I have to do, but what I want to do. To be able to read three novels a week, write a book, spend more time with my husband, with my son. In the time that I do have, I have everything that is important to me—most of the time."

. . .

Sally Quinn, former reporter for *The Washington Post* and author of the best-selling novel *Regrets Only,* says, "I don't think it's possible to have a totally successful career, be a wonderful mother and have a fabulous marriage all at the same time. Something has to be sacrificed. Somewhere along the line something has to give.

"When I was writing my book, my son came first, my husband came second and the book came last. But when the book came out and I had to promote it, the book came first, my son second and Ben third. And I'll tell you something. They were not happy. And because they weren't happy, I wasn't happy. When I put the book first, they were the ones who sacrificed and suffered. At this point in my life, I would rather put them first and my writing third, because ultimately that is what makes me the happiest.

"I don't know anyone who does all three brilliantly. Every time I see some smug woman sitting there saying, 'Oh, well, I do have it all, and what can I say?' it just makes me crazy. They are just trying to make it seem that way. It is not fair to make women think it is possible to do all this without somebody getting shortchanged."

"When it comes to having it all, I have it all as far as names go," says Ponce Kiah Marchelle Heloise Cruse Evans, whom most of us know as Heloise, the columnist who has answers for just about every household problem.

"When you are talking about can you really have it all, you have to ask yourself, What is 'it all'? Is it great financial security? Or recognition? Being the president of a corporation or landing the biggest advertising contract?

"And where will your husband and children fit in? I can remember when my mother didn't get there for things like my seventh-grade graduation, because she was lecturing or something. At the time, I didn't understand. Now, as an adult, I do. But women are going to run into those times when their child looks at them with tears in her eyes and says, 'Why are you leaving me?' when you go on tour or 'Why aren't you coming to my school play?'

"I tell those women who want it all to ask someone who had it all to tell them the truth. What it is really like. Going without sleep. Scrubbing the floor at four in the morning. Typing your report after everyone else has gone to bed. Going to work leaving a sick child with a sitter and being sick on your feet yourself. That kind of thing. Is it really worth it? Remember when Ann Landers asked her readers, 'If you had it to do all over again, would you have children?' And the overwhelming majority said *No!*"

Barbara Hendricks, the concert and opera singer who lives in Switzerland with her husband and two children and commutes to engagements in Europe and the United States, says, "I think when people want to have it all, they want it to run like honey. Life is not like that. Having it all does not mean that your children will not go through difficult periods, that your marriage relationship will not be strained at times, that your career will not have its ups and downs.

"It was not easy for me to make certain choices, but that is what life is about—making choices and dealing with the consequences. Whatever choices we make, we are dealing with other human beings. This means we have a responsibility to be attentive, to be aware. That takes a lot of time and a lot of energy. You also must realize that it is an investment, which means you have to put something into it. And that is the part that is not easy.

"I feel I have to be very aware of my husband, my children and my public so that no one is cheated. Sometimes I have to fight the urge to do everything perfectly. I have to realize that what I give to my children, to my husband, is that I am a human being with all the imperfections that make me lovable."

"I feel that I have what I want—although I wouldn't use the phrase 'have it all,' because I think it is arrogant," says

Karen Nussbaum, executive director of Nine to Five, a national association of working women, and president of District 925 Service Employees International Union in Cleveland, Ohio.

"I feel satisfied with the choices I've made, but I do wish I had more time. I wish I was enthralled with the child care that my children have. I wish I never had to rush home and find there's nothing in the house for dinner and have to give the kids peanut-butter sandwiches again. I wish that I never had to work another weekend in my life. I wish I didn't have to do my own shopping or my own cleaning, but I do. And I feel that it is a small price to pay for all the satisfaction I get from my family and my work."

"Most of us have trouble juggling," says Barbara Walters of ABC News. "The woman who says that she doesn't is someone whom I admire but have never met. The fewer responsibilities you have, obviously the easier it is to conduct your career successfully. It is much easier to juggle a marriage and a career than to juggle a marriage, a career and a child.

"I remember talking to Margaret Mead, the anthropologist, years ago. She was talking about how her graduate students would come to her and complain about how hard it was—marriage and children and work—and why hadn't anybody told them that it was going to be so hard? And Margaret Mead replied, 'Who says that you can have it all at the same time?' "

And then there is Helen Gurley Brown, the supersuccessful editor of *Cosmopolitan* magazine. "There is a lot of propaganda aimed at women now, trying to get them not to have it all, to just lean back a little and smell the daisies and don't try to be a CEO. It is up to the woman what she really wants. Yes, it is a lot of hard work. Yes, you do make some sacrifices. But frankly, I can't remember any I've made. I never wanted to have children.

"I think you *can* have it all, but you obviously have to work very hard and be well organized and have a husband who will cooperate. There are women—*Cosmo* women—everywhere who are doing it."

I will tell you a secret. I don't believe in the Tooth Fairy. I don't believe in Santa Claus. And I especially don't believe in Superwoman. Superwoman is a myth. She is the symbol of that fraudulent bill of goods that women have been sold. I was delighted when Vesna Prija, a Yugoslav journalist who addressed an International Women's Media Conference, put the Superwoman myth in perspective. "I have never met a man in my life," she said, "who felt bad because he was not an ideal husband and an ideal father and extraordinarily successful in his career. So why should we women be captive of this myth?"

Feminist Gloria Steinem explains the Superwoman myth this way. "Superwoman was the response of a reluctant society saying, 'Okay, you can be a lawyer or a carpenter if you want to, but only if you keep preparing three meals a day, take care of the kids and don't disturb the order of things as they are.' No feminist ever said we should be Superwomen. No one has any right to expect us to be."

And no one can be. After a ten-year study of women physicians, psychologist Lillian Kaufman Cartwright concluded that any woman who tries to be Superwoman is going to drive herself crazy.

Cartwright interviewed and tested 58 women entering the University of California Medical School in San Francisco between 1964 and 1967. All of them scored high in self-esteem, self-acceptance and dominance. She did a follow-up study on 49 of the women between 1974 and 1977. By that time 75 percent of them were married, 12 percent were divorced and 50 percent had children.

Almost 90 percent of the women were satisfied with their medical careers. But over half of them also said that they found trying to balance career and home life stressful. Twenty percent found it extremely stressful. Four percent reported that they had reached the breaking point.

Only 20 percent reported no significant stress.

The breaking-point women were markedly different from the others. They felt that they must be perfect wives, perfect mothers and perfect doctors. They had more children than the other mothers in the study—as many as they would have had if they had not chosen to have a career. They tried to be full-time mothers as well as full-time physicians.

The women who reported no significant stress had set priorities for themselves. They had decided what they wanted most. For some, career came first. For others it was family.

The career-oriented women had only one child—or none at all. (Other studies have shown that 60 percent of married women executives have no children.) They delegated as many of their family responsibilities as possible.

The family-oriented arranged their careers so that they would not interfere with family responsibilities. They made no apologies for taking a week off because Amanda had chicken pox or Jeffrey was having his tonsils out.

The happiest—and healthiest—women, psychologist Cartwright concluded, are not the women who try to do *everything* perfectly, but the ones who decide what is most important to them and go all out to do it well. If their career is most important, they don't fret about dust kittens under the beds or feel that they must be gourmet cooks. If their family is most important, they do not consider themselves failures if they do not rise to the top of their profession.

The woman who really wants it can have a good marriage and a satisfying career and bring up emotionally healthy children if she establishes her priorities and refuses to torture herself by trying to be a superwife, a supersuccess and a supermother.

I know this. Not only because studies like Cartwright's

prove it, but because my mother has done it. I have done it. And my daughter is doing it. It is not easy. It can be a ghastly grind at times, stressful to both mind and body, but the rewards are tremendous. Even knowing what I know today about the costs of juggling career and family, I would do it all over again. All of it. Happily.

THREE

I THINK of my mother as every bit as much a pioneer as the men and women who colonized the American frontier or the astronauts who took that "giant step for mankind" on the moon.

She was a devoted wife and mother—and a successful lawyer—at a time when a married woman in one of the professions was a rare bird indeed. One of her former colleagues at the bar told me recently that Mother had a mind like quicksilver. "It was next to impossible to keep up with her," he said. "In a case involving a clear-cut legal issue, I would suddenly find myself arguing against apple pie and motherhood and democracy without quite understanding how she had maneuvered me into such a position." Mother was known for her ability to win cases that were considered hopeless; but her life was centered around her family.

Her marriage was everything to her. She started going with my father when she was fifteen and he was sixteen. There was never anyone else for either of them. They went

to law school at the same time. After they were married, they
went to the office together every day until shortly before his
death. They were never apart for more than a few hours at
a time during the fifty years of their marriage.

Mother would come home from the office, kiss my sister
Elaine and me and go straight to the kitchen to get supper.
Never anything fancy. We used to tease her that she was a
great short-order cook. She and my father used to stop at
the Automat on their way home to pick up meat loaf or beef
stew or a dessert so often that Elaine and I used to call the
Automat "Mother's."

She never sat down at the dinner table. She stood at one
end of the table and served everyone. She did her eating on
the run, always bustling in and out of the kitchen.

Despite Mother's legal career, Elaine and I never felt neglected. When we were sick, she was there. (My father would
never have dreamed of staying home, nor would she have
asked him to—or even thought of asking him.) When we had
a problem, she was there.

And she was always there for my father. Her role in life, the
one she chose and loved, was to make his life easier—at home
and at the office. She thought of herself as his right hand.

I was grown up when I realized that my parents, who were
partners in everything else, were not law partners. It was my
father's law practice, not *their* practice. When I discovered
this, I told Dad I thought it was terribly unfair. He was upset.
It had never occurred to him to make Mother a partner. He
happily went to work and had partnership papers drawn up
and new stationery printed—and then he told Mother about
it as a surprise.

And you know what my mother said?

She said, "No, thank you, dear."

She always wanted my father to feel that he was in charge.
"I was happy to submerge my personality in his," she told
an interviewer after Dad died. "We were always very much
in love."

When I asked Mother if she had any regrets, if she would

change anything if she had those years to live over, she shook her head. "Not one thing," she said firmly. But then after a moment she said, "Well, yes, there are regrets. I regret that your father and I had only fifty years together. And I regret that we did not have a big party for our fiftieth anniversary. But you know your father. He didn't want people to know that he was old enough to have been married fifty years." She smiled indulgently.

As I think back over her life, I realize that during all her married life, she lacked one important thing: friends. Her life was so filled by her work, her husband and her children that there was no time left for friendship. Very little time for anything.

I doubt that my mother ever had a moment while Elaine and I were growing up that she could call her own. No time to curl up with a novel, to go for a long walk, to be quiet for a while and let the world go by.

She has time in abundance now. After she recovered from the shock of my father's death, she began filling her life with friends. She now has more than enough time—time to read, to watch television, to visit her children and grandchildren. As she always told me, "There is a time for everything."

All my married life I have felt like a juggler with a dozen balls in the air. I work long hours at my multiple careers as psychological journalist, columnist, author, lecturer, consultant to industry groups and occasional actress. I work at being a good daughter, mother and grandmother. I work hardest of all at my marriage, because it is the most important part of my life.

After thirty-eight years of juggling marriage and work and motherhood, I am neither weary nor burnt out. I love every minute of my life—even those predawn hours when I come dragging home after a full day's work in Los Angeles followed by an overnight transcontinental flight so that I can get breakfast for Milt. His pleasure at having me across the breakfast table, even after all these years, makes it well worthwhile.

We have had our ups and downs. Our marriage, like most marriages, has been a constant series of negotiations and compromises between Milt's career and mine, between our differing theories of child-rearing, between our completely different ideas of what constitutes a good time, and a thousand other issues.

We have had to cope with the fact that I make significantly more money than he does, with the fact that as a physician he has more or less regular hours, while I spend half my days flying around the country from one engagement to another and am not able to get home every night. We have had to negotiate the fact that Milt loves parties, loves nothing more than inviting half a dozen people home for dinner on the spur of the moment, whereas my idea of a wonderful time is a quiet evening together at home talking and watching television.

My work is stimulating emotionally, and financially rewarding. I have a good marriage, a wonderful husband, a beloved daughter, enchanting grandchildren. But do I have it all? No, I don't. I have my share of regrets: sometimes, I think, more than my share.

I probably regret most of all the times Lisa felt I let her down. Time after time, when she was growing up, I would clear a day for something that was important to her. And then something would come up. I always fulfilled the times I promised her, but there were gray areas when I said I would "try my best" to be there. Even though Milt would try to attend the school play or the gymkhana or whatever, she always resented that my career took priority over some of her big moments.

It is only now when she is in the same position of occasionally having to disappoint her own children that she understands that there are some things that you just can't deal with. But it still hurts her.

A few months ago, Milt and I had a big family party. We had planned it for weeks. There were forty-nine of us altogether, including Lisa and her husband and children. But that night, I had to leave shortly after dinner when the kids were in bed to make an eleven o'clock plane to Los Angeles, where I was scheduled to do a television show the next day. I was home again within twenty-four hours, and Lisa and the children were still there, so that we had time to visit together the next day. But when she left to go back to Iowa, she said wistfully, "I wish you hadn't had to leave." And my stress level zoomed up all over again—even though I knew she understood.

In fact, every time I plan something that involves Lisa, I am filled with an incredible amount of anxiety until the moment when we are actually together. Every time the telephone rings beforehand, I have a quiver of terror that it may be something that will force me to cancel whatever we had planned.

At the same time, I regret all the career opportunities to which I have said no. When I did turn down a project because Lisa had a school play or a recital, I always resented it internally. I always thought it might have been the golden opportunity for a breakthrough into something new.

A few years ago, for instance, I was asked to be in a film with David Bowie and Catherine Deneuve and Susan Sarandon. I would be playing a television reporter. I was really interested. This would be a new frontier for me. I mentioned it to someone quite casually and he said, "Oh, that's the one all about lesbians and vampires." Well! That, I thought, was not for me. I did not want Milt or Lisa or my grandchildren to be embarrassed by anything I did, so I bowed out.

As it turned out, *The Hunger* was an excellent film, sensitively acted and directed. It received very good reviews. I have always kicked myself that I didn't ask a few more questions before turning it down.

I also regret that, like my mother, I have no intimate friends. My life is so hectic that I do not have the time to invest that friendship requires. I know hundreds and hundreds of peo-

ple, but I have no close friends. This is a deficit in my life.
I think the majority of successful women suffer the same
deficit.

Susan Waterfall, director of the investment firm Forst-
mann-Leff in New York City, says, "I wish I had more time
for women friends. That's the one thing I really miss." And
when British Prime Minister Margaret Thatcher was asked
if she had any friends, she said, "There is so much when you
are in politics that you must not say, and you cannot say, that
maintaining a friendship is difficult." Then she smiled. "But
I have a family that is absolutely marvelous." I feel the same
way. Milt is my best friend. And I can share my worries and
triumphs with my sister Elaine, knowing that she will sym-
pathize and rejoice along with me.

I regret every night I have had to spend away from my
husband—and I spend at least one night a week away from
home. On the other hand, this particular cloud seems to have
its own silver lining. My time with Milt is more special simply
because I am not there all the time. "It's more fun when
you're home," he tells me. And I like that. Our marriage has
never had a chance to get stale.

My daughter Lisa's life resembles that of her grandparents
in one way. She and her husband, both ophthalmologists,
have a joint practice and go to work together every morning
and come home together every night.

Right now, as a wife and mother and physician, she probably is going through the most pressured time of her life.
With three young children, she is often worn to a frazzle.

There are days, she says, when she looks forward to going
to work and getting away from the demands of the house
and the children. She finds the quiet discipline of eye surgery
both challenging and relaxing. At the end of the day, she is
eager to get back to the children.

"Do you have any regrets?" I asked her.

"I regret that there are not six more hours in the day,"
she said. "I don't have enough time with my husband. I don't

have enough time with my children. I don't even have time to cut my toenails. I'm too busy cutting everyone else's."

Lisa is a happy woman. She radiates happiness, but she certainly does not have it all. When I asked her if she felt she did, she laughed.

"Have all what?" she asked. "I feel as if I'm treading water night and day. If I can just keep my head above water for the next few years, I'll consider myself a successful woman. Right now the name of the game is survival."

Because my mother had done it, it was easier for me to combine work and marriage and motherhood. And for Lisa, who grew up with the examples of both her mother and grandmother, it seems only natural. I don't think my daughter ever envisaged a life for herself that did not include marriage and children and work.

The three generations of dual-career marriages in our family are quite unusual. Even today, *two* generations of dual-career marriages are the exception rather than the norm. Having a role model helps.

For first-generation dual-careerists, there are scores of role models in this book, women who are juggling careers and marriages and who tell just how they are doing it and what they have learned in the process.

I consider them all successful women. Some are famous. Others are known only to their colleagues and their families. They have talked frankly about money, sex, guilt, husbands and lovers, fatigue, resentment, frustration, triumphs and satisfactions, the ups and downs of their lives.

Not every woman's solutions are going to be right for you; but I think you will find that many of the compromises, the trade-offs, the strategies and the attitudes these women reveal can be adapted to your own life to help you get—and keep—what you want most.

FOUR

MY MOTHER, my daughter and I put marriage first in our lives without even having to think about it. Marriage was the fulcrum of my mother's existence for half a century. Marriage creates an environment in which my daughter and I thrive. I tell my lecture audiences that marriage is the salt of daily life. It makes everything a little bit better. Knowing that you are the most important person in someone else's life is the source of happiness and security and just plain well-being. There is nothing else like it.

Unfortunately, many dual-career marriages are an uneasy union of resentful wife and dissatisfied husband. For every good marriage, there is more than one bad one.

It does not have to be this way. Marriage has changed. It is not what it used to be. And I think this is good. Good for women, at any rate. It can be equally good for men if they learn to adjust to the changes. The woman who understands the new psychological forces at work in dual-career marriages and how they affect the man she loves can help make his adjustment easier—and her marriage more joyful.

The core problem women face in combining career and marriage is, quite simply, their husbands. Their husbands' attitudes. Expectations. Fears. Insecurities. Even those men who profess to believe that work and marriage, personal achievement and family are no more incompatible for their wives than they are for themselves often conceal fear and hostility that surface at times of stress and simmer quietly and unhealthily the rest of the time. Anthony Astrachan, author of *How Men Feel: Their Response to Women's Demands for Equality and Power*, estimates on the basis of his research that no more than 5 or 10 percent of the married male population has wholeheartedly accepted the role of equal partner in marriage.

The fact is that there are precious few equal-opportunity marriages. But there are some. And there can be more.

The first step in combining marriage and career harmoniously and constructively is to understand just how enormously marriage has changed since the 1950s. Those were the storybook days of Mom and Dad and Dick and Jane and their dog Spot. When things were the way they were supposed to be. When Dad went to work and Mom stayed home and took care of the house and the kids. When Dad was King of the Castle. And they all lived happily ever after.

At least, that was the way the story went. That was the way it was in the movies and in the women's magazines. But in real life, things were different. Especially for Mom. Mom was finding out that marriage was not the state of automatic bliss she had been led to expect. It was definitely not a case of living happily ever after.

Mirror, mirror on the wall,
Who is the happiest one of all?

A psychologist asked himself this question, although perhaps not in the same words, in those prefeminist days. And then he set out to sift through the accumulated research on happiness to find an answer.

As he pored over study after study on happiness, he became convinced that women had a far greater capacity for happiness than men. He based his conclusion on the evidence of studies that showed women were more flexible than men and that women had more realistic expectations about life than men and that women expressed their emotions more easily than men. Eventually he was able to construct a composite profile of the person most likely to be happy.

A woman. Of course.

This happy woman was between the ages of twenty-eight and forty-eight. She was a woman of average intelligence. She was a woman who had too much to do. She was, in short, a married woman.

The psychologist's long hours of research had paid off. He had discovered a significant difference between the sexes. There was just one problem. Married women may have had the greatest potential for happiness, but major studies revealed that in actuality married *men* were the happiest people of all.

This was first established by a landmark study that rocked the whole community of social scientists and mental-health professionals back on their heels when it was published in 1960, because of what it revealed about marriage. A team of researchers at the University of Michigan's Survey Research Center had interviewed more than 2,500 men and women, a carefully selected cross-section of Americans, to find out how happy they thought they were.

What they discovered when it came to marriage was a shocker. More than half the married people they interviewed said that their marriages were unhappy. And almost all of those unhappily married souls were women. Most of the men reported that they were extremely satisfied with their marriages.

When the researchers analyzed their findings on how happy

Americans considered themselves, they found that the happiest people of all were married men. The next-happiest were single women. Married women were third. And then came the bachelors.

How could this be true if married women had such a significantly higher potential for happiness than men?

"Women have more invested in their marriages. Marriage and home are more central to the woman's life," the Michigan group wrote. And this had led women to have greater expectations of marriage than their husbands. "Their lower degree of happiness is an indication that these expectations are not being fulfilled."

Ten years later, the U.S. Department of Health, Education and Welfare carried out a similar large-scale study that yielded similar results. Nothing had changed. Married men were still the winner's in the happiness sweepstakes. And married women were still a dreary third.

What these studies suggested was that well over half the married women in the country were suffering from an identity crisis brought on by the fact that technology had rendered much of the married woman's traditional role obsolete. In one of my columns on the subject at the time, I quoted a diary entry made by a Philadelphian in 1778.

"From early in the morning till late at night," this gentleman wrote, "my wife is constantly employed in affairs of the family. This calls for her constant attendance in the kitchen, baking our bread and pies and meat, her cleanliness about the house, her attendance in the orchard cutting and drying of apples; her seeing to all our washing done. Add to this her making of twenty large cheeses, besides her sewing, knitting . . ." And undoubtedly the care and education of a brood of children.

Women's work was never done in those days. Wives were an important part of the family economic unit. The wife was a hands-on executive, a manager. But by the 1950s, wives were no longer helpmates and partners, but dependents.

Their work, although it still kept many of them bustling from morning to night, was largely made work. Technology had reduced their role to serving their husbands and rearing the children. That 1950s Mom of Dick and Jane was usually working and living far below her capacity. The single working woman, although considered somewhat of a second-class citizen because of her inability to catch a man, was happier. She was self-supporting, in control of her life. She might be lonely, but quite possibly not as lonely as her married sister.

"We all have capacities clamoring to be used," taught the eminent psychologist Abraham Maslow. "We crave self-actualization, to make the most of the abilities we possess."

Felice Schwartz, sixty-two, president of Catalyst, a national research and advisory organization that fosters the career and leadership development of women, says, "I think for my generation, the lucky women were those who just loved being at home full time with their children. And very few women did."

Those women whose capacities were fulfilled by marriage and children were a minority, according to the studies. Women who needed more, wanted more, were for the most part stymied. Marriage was not enough for them, but what else was there? When Milt and I were married in the 1950s, married women who, like me, pursued a career were rarities. It was a man's world. He was the head of his family. His word was law. His home was his castle and he was king. That is the way marriage was at the turn of the half-century and for most of the next quarter-century.

But enough of history. What of marriage today?

Well, for one thing, that storybook family—Mom and Dad, Dick and Jane and faithful old Spot—is an endangered species today, as imperiled as the condor or the whooping crane. In 1986, families with a father who worked and a mother who stayed home were less than 10 percent of American families.

There have been no recent major studies like the 1960

Michigan survey and the 1970 HEW study, but a group of smaller studies indicates very strongly that the pendulum has swung, that by and large women are the happiest people now. Married women. Married women who work outside the home.

Two recent studies, one of a group of 197 women and another of 96 women, were carried out by researchers at Columbia University's School of Medicine and Boston Unviersity's Department of Psychology to explore how women were coping with their life choices. They categorized these life choices as—

1. Single and at home
2. Single and working
3. Married and at home
4. Married and working

The women who had chosen the multiple roles of wife, mother and working woman tended to be the happiest and healthiest. They seemed to thrive on their busy, stress-filled lives. In descending order of physical and emotional health came single working women, married women who stayed at home and finally single women who stayed at home.

A third study, this one of 232 professional women—doctors, lawyers and professors—in and around Philadelphia, found that although 77 percent of the women reported difficulties in combining marriage and career, 85 percent of them were happy with their lives. Only 15 percent were dissatisfied.

In 1986, *The Wall Street Journal* in combination with the Gallup organization did a survey focusing on some 700 women in top management. They found that the married women executives were happier than the single women.

The difference between the findings of these four surveys of women and those of a survey, by the American Management Association, of 2,800 top male business executives is striking.

A startling number of these men—83 percent of them—reported that they were not happy with their lives. They spoke of wanting a chance for self-expression, of wanting to be more involved with their families, of wanting to fulfill their potential. It was not that they hated their work, but it was no longer enough for them. They were no longer willing to be consumed by it. They wanted to be free to channel their drives in other directions that they considered more emotionally rewarding.

In a way, these men were like the 1950s wives who had embraced marriage and homemaking and child rearing with enthusiasm and dedication—only to find that that was not enough. Like the 1950s wives, these top male executives were saying, "There must be more. This is not enough."

Another study, designed by psychologists at the University of Michigan to find out how married women's jobs affected their husbands, discovered that the men whose wives worked were not as psychologically whole nor as physically healthy as those whose wives stayed home.

The pendulum seems to have swung. The married woman who works has come into her own at last. Her potential for happiness is finally being fulfilled. And with close to two-thirds of married women working outside the home, it seems that the majority of married women are happier than married men these days.

Why should this be? It would seem that men would be relieved that they no longer have to carry the financial burden of the family alone, especially since the cost of maintaining a home and raising a family is more than the average man earns. Seventy percent of married couples who buy a house these days need two salaries to handle the mortgage payments, insurance, taxes and upkeep. Couples who want children, a house of their own, a car, vacations and all the rest of basic middle-class expectations cannot afford them without two paychecks.

Since this is the case, why do men react so negatively to

their wife's working outside the home? What is it about her working that eats away at them physically and psychologically? And why are they not happy that their wives are stimulated and challenged by their jobs and are using their full capacities, living in high gear?

Some answers to these questions were suggested by a recent study, by a Rutgers University team, of more than 1,500 married men which established that husbands whose wives worked were less satisfied with both their home and work lives than husbands with stay-home wives.

Over and over, the men with working wives told the researchers that they felt inadequate. This feeling of inadequacy held true no matter how old the man was, how much he earned (or how much his wife earned), whether or not he had gone to college, whether he held a white-collar or blue-collar position.

"This perception of their inadequacy as family bread-winners is a central component of their mental health," the researchers wrote. "Men must broaden their conception of what it means to be a good provider. They must understand that they are not solely responsible for providing for the family."

The men's responses also reflected feelings of hostility, resentment and a profound uneasiness about what they saw as an erosion of power and privilege. They felt diminished because they no longer enjoyed the status and services their fathers had taken for granted.

In other words, these husbands were going through an identity crisis similar to the crisis married women went through in the 1950s and 1960s. Their roles have changed. They are no longer kings of the castle, no longer heads of the household—except in the eyes of the Internal Revenue Service.

You, as a working wife, must understand that your husband may feel beleaguered and inadequate, even though he may not show it, even if he insists he is totally supportive of your career. You have more than women have ever had—

status, money and the independence that a paycheck confers. He believes he has less than men have ever had.

Marriage does not have to be a seesaw with one partner up and the other down, one frustrated and the other fulfilled, one happy and the other unhappy. It is time to get off this marital teeter-totter, to establish a loving relationship in which both partners can be happy and flourish.

You will have to give more than he does, do more than he does. But you have more to give—and more to gain. Now that you understand just how rapid and revolutionary the changes in the power structure of marriage have been, you can work on your own marriage so that your husband will find his dual-career marriage more exciting, more sharing and more loving than his father's traditional marriage.

Other women have done it. You can too. In the following chapters, I will tell you what I have done to keep my marriage flourishing. And what other women have done. The psychological tools for constructing a happy marriage will be yours to use as you think best.

PART TWO

MAKING CHOICES

FIVE

THE MOST important advice I can give a woman when it comes to juggling career and marriage is to put herself first.

Selfish?

Not at all. After all, whose life is it? It is yours, the only one you have. If you are going to make the most of it, then you must live it the way that is best for you.

When I say put yourself first, I am talking about what psychologist Abraham Maslow called self-actualization: making the most of yourself and your abilities, not sacrificing yourself by not living up to your potential.

"If you make a choice thinking you are making a sacrifice, sacrificing something because of family or career or whatever, then you become unhappy," says Japanese-born Jun Kanai, U.S. representative of Issey Miyake, the Japanese couture designer, and mother of two children, aged thirteen and eight.

"The minute you start thinking, 'I'm sacrificing my next trip to Paris, or my promotion, because of the kids,' then it becomes self-pity. I don't think I sacrifice anything. Whenever I made a choice, it was because I preferred it that way." Jun Kanai fits the self-actualizer profile developed by North Carolina psychologist Alvin Jones and Dr. Rick Crandall, editor of the *Journal of Social Behavior and Personality*. It depicts self-actualizers as knowing what they want out of life, feeling responsible both for themselves and for others and radiating self-esteem. They are guided by their own standards rather than those of others. They are here-and-now–oriented, doing the very best they can at the moment, but also keeping their goals in sight. They find life a challenge and a pleasure.

Karol Emmerich, who leads a high-pressure life as executive, wife and mother, stresses the spiritual side to putting oneself first.

"Balance is important," she says. "Not tying up your whole sense of self-worth in the job. Or in your husband. Being married has been great. Being a mom is great. My job is great. But I think you need to find a sense of self so that you don't need any of those things to feel good about yourself.

"In my own case, my religion has played a big role. It is probably the major reason for my being successful, because it has given me peace and self-confidence and the ability to deal with stress."

You cannot put yourself first unless you know what you want out of life. "You have to know your priorities," says comedian Joan Rivers.

When I interviewed Joan shortly before the death of her husband, she told me, "The most important things to me are my child, my marriage (which means my husband), my career and then my home. I know exactly what is important to me.

"If they should say, 'Come home from the studio, your house is on fire,' I'd say, 'Let it burn.' But if they were to say, 'Come home from the studio, your husband is sick,' I wouldn't go back to the studio until he was well. When Edgar had his heart attack, I didn't want to hear, 'You gotta do the Carson show.' But if the house had burned down, I would have said, 'I can still manage the Carson show.' "

"You have to think, 'What do I want?' " says Julia Child, who almost single-handedly taught Americans to master French cooking. Happy with her life as wife of a Foreign Service officer ("I was Paul's wife and baggage"), she had never considered a career "until I was thirty-five and discovered cooking. And that was that. Everything changed."

When asked if she regretted her former life, she said matter-of-factly, "If you are going to have a career, there are certain things you are going to have to give up. I rarely go out to lunch because it takes up so much time. I have a big pile of books I want to read, but I never get to read. I'd like to do more museum work and play more golf, that kind of thing, but I have very little time.

"I enjoy my career," she emphasized. "It's what I want. You have to get a perfectly clear picture of what you want out of life. You are not going to get it all. You have to decide what gives you most satisfaction."

It is not easy, this business of knowing what will give you the most satisfaction. The famous psychiatrist Dr. Roy Menninger used to ask new patients, "Does your use of your vital resources truly reflect your priorities?" Most people answered yes, but when they learned to know themselves better, 90 percent of them changed their answers to no.

How about you? Does your use of your vital resources and abilities truly reflect your priorities? What *are* your priorities? What do you really want most out of life?

Knowing yourself is not easy. We are affected more than we realize by images of ourselves reflected by friends and family and coworkers. We tend to go along with their assessments without examining the very real possibility that they may be wrong.

This happened to me. I did not grow up wanting to be a

psychologist. My secret wish was to be in show business. But those were the days of the glamour stars—Rita Hayworth and Paulette Goddard, Ginger Rogers and Claudette Colbert. I was attractive enough, with the scrubbed look of the nice girl next door, but I was not glamorous. I was afraid I didn't have a chance.

So being practical, I decided to become a psychologist. This was something that interested me very much. I had very definite goals. I wanted to be a professor of psychology at a major university, and I also wanted to be a good wife and mother. At Cornell, I took a double major, home economics and psychology, so I could be as well prepared for domestic life as for professional life.

But every time I went to the movies, I could see myself up there on the screen, a star. After Milt and I were married, I auditioned for several television shows. I thought that if I did get a role, I could still continue working for my doctorate in psychology at Columbia.

All I got was turndowns. The final one was the most devastating. My mother-in-law had a good friend who was head of an advertising agency and had considerable clout in the television world. As a favor to her, he agreed to see me. I asked him if he could advise me on how to break into show business.

"Joyce, go home," he said. "Be a good wife and have nice kids. You have no chance in a million years. Forget it."

And that was that. Right from the shoulder. I stopped auditioning for television roles. But I will tell you right now that it was the last time I took no for an answer without challenging it.

Then *The Sixty-four Thousand Dollar Question* came along. For those of you who were not watching television in 1955, it was a quiz show. Not just a quiz show, but the hottest show on television. On Tuesday nights, everyone watched *The Sixty-four,* following the efforts of contestants to win the $64,000, which was a fortune at that time. The more I watched it, the more I thought, "I could do that."

I did not think of it in terms of show business. What I was thinking about was money. I had stopped teaching and doing research when Lisa was born. As a psychologist, I was convinced of the importance of full-time mothering for the first three years. Now I was ready to get back to work.

Not only had I had enough of staying home (I was climbing the walls with boredom), we were broke. We were living on Milt's salary as a hospital resident: $50 a month. It went a lot further in those days, but not far enough.

I did not even dream of winning the $64,000. My goal was a smaller prize—the Cadillac. If I could win the Cadillac, Milt and I could drive around in it all summer. Show off to our friends. Go to the beach. Visit my folks in the country. And when winter came, we would sell it and have a nice little nest egg.

I analyzed the show. All the contestants were similar in one respect. There was a shoemaker who knew all about opera, for instance, and there was a burly Marine who was a gourmet cook. Every contestant had a built-in incongruity.

I was short and blond and pretty, a psychologist and the mother of an almost-three-year-old. There was nothing paradoxical about me, nothing that would catch the attention of the powers-that-be that cast the quiz show. After some thought, I decided to become an expert on either plumbing or boxing. Either would be sufficiently incongruous with my image. Milt advised me to go with boxing. "No one wants to hear about stopped-up toilets," he said. So I went to work to turn myself into a boxing expert. I ate, drank and slept boxing—its history, its statistics, its personalities.

When I felt I was ready, I applied for the show and was accepted. I went on and won. I kept on winning. I was on every week. I loved being in front of the television cameras. And one night, I won big. I won the $64,000!

It changed my life. I was on television and radio. I was making personal appearances. I was in show business! My two interests, show business and psychology, dovetailed as if

I had been planning this kind of career ever since I was a freshman in college. But I had not.

It was not until after I won *The Sixty-four* that I even dreamed of a career as a psychological journalist, working in front of television cameras and translating the results of psychological research into terms that people could use in their everyday lives. At the time, there was no such job description. Once I glimpsed the possibility of what I could be, however, there was no stopping me. It was what I wanted more than anything else in the world. I shiver sometimes when I think I almost missed out because I believed that man who told me to "go home and be a good wife."

When I look back, I realize that unless I had really loved the idea of appearing on television in front of an audience of hundreds of thousands, I would never have considered trying out for *The Sixty-four*. So, while it was the Cadillac that I wanted, there was an unconscious inner force pushing me on, saying, "I want to be in show business. This might be my chance."

The moral of this little story is that you cannot let other people's opinions stop you from trying to do what you want.

The big problem for most people is finding out what they really do want. An experiment with chimpanzees sheds some light on this business of learning to know ourselves. Four chimpanzees that had been born in the wild were placed in four empty rooms. After a couple of days, a mirror was propped up in each room. Researchers observed the animals' reactions through observation holes in the walls.

The immediate reaction was hostility. Each of the four seemed to believe his reflection was a stranger, an enemy. Each made fierce noises and put on a show of belligerence.

After three days their behavior began to change. Each animal slowly came to understand that he was not looking at an enemy but at himself. At this point their behavior changed dramatically. They no longer threatened their reflections, but observed them with interest. They watched themselves chewing their food. They looked in the mirror when they groomed themselves. They liked to watch themselves blow bubbles. With each succeeding day, they became more and more aware of themselves.

A mirror is not going to help you learn anything about yourself that you do not know already; but there are psychological mirrors you can use to see yourself free of the distortions of other people's opinions and expectations, free of your own illusions about yourself.

A most effective psychological tool for discovering what you really want out of life is the Goal Analysis. You do not need a psychologist for this. All you need is a couple of hours to yourself, pen and paper and the desire to know more about yourself. The Goal Analysis consists of writing down the answers to the four questions that follow.

CAREER GOALS

1. Where do you want to be in your business or professional life ten years from now?

Be specific. And realistic. Don't put down President of the United States, for instance, if you have never been active in politics. What position do you want to hold? What title do you want to have? How much money do you want to be making? How autonomous do you want to be? What kind of company or organization do you want to be working for? Or do you want to be your own boss? Do you want a corner office? A chauffeur-driven limousine to take you to work and home again? Do you want fame? Status? Political power? Riches?

Make a list of everything you want to have achieved in your career by the end of a decade. Don't confine yourself to these few questions. They are just to start you thinking.

2. Where do you want to be in your business or professional life one year from now?

Be even more specific here. Do you want a promotion? What kind? A new job? What? A raise? How much? Do you want to work toward a graduate degree in your field of interest? Transfer to another part of the country? Where? Take up a completely different line of work? What?

PERSONAL GOALS

1. What do you want your personal life to be like ten years from now?

Do you want to be married? Divorced from your present husband? Have children? How many? Where do you want to live? Suburbs? Country? City? Another part of the country? Another country? What kind of lifestyle do you want to have? Do you want to share more activities with your husband? Travel? Do you want to collect art? Have a lover? Belong to the country club?

Write it all down, a picture of your life as you would like it to be in another ten years.

2. What do you want your personal life to be like a year from now?

Do you want to get married? Have a relationship? Break up with the current man in your life? Fall in love? Do you want to get pregnant? Have a face lift? Move? Make more friends? Give up smoking? Find someone dependable to take care of the baby? Lose fifteen pounds? Stop your family from interfering in your life? Have your husband do his share around the house? Buy a house? Be more independent?

When you finish you should have a detailed description of what you would like your life to be like twelve months from now.

And that is it for the time being. Put your analysis away in a safe place for two weeks; then set aside a couple of hours to go over it. You will probably want to make changes. Even if you have not given any thought to your analysis during these two weeks, your brain has been working away on it, assessing what you have written, making additions and deletions. Freud called this process "the unconscious at work."

Make whatever changes you want, and then decide on the one goal that means most to you in each of the four groups. Write down the two most important personal goals and the two most important career goals. Next, decide which set of goals is more important to you. If push came to shove, would you dump the personal goals for the career goals? Or vice versa?

Add these choices to your Goal Analysis. You know more about yourself now than you did two weeks ago. You are aware of what you want out of life. When you are faced with choices, you can make your decision on an informed basis. You know what you want. You can put yourself first.

Carole Sinclair, forty-four, cofounder, publisher and editorial director of *Sylvia Porter's Personal Finance Magazine*, has learned that her life works best when she puts herself first. Strongly goal-oriented, she has also discovered that her goals change.

"The trick is having what you need when you need it, as opposed to trying to come up with something that is going to last forever. When I was twenty-two, I would have felt like an absolute wallflower if I hadn't had a husband. Today, my first priority is my daughter and the second is my job.

"My needs are so different now from what they were ten years ago, or five years ago! I just try and be honest with myself about what will put a smile on my face and make me feel good. And then I go do it. I think having it all is having what you need at the time."

Carole is quite right. Do not let yourself become a captive

of your goals. A goal is nothing more nor less than a guide to your future—and a temporary guide at that. You are going to change and your goals will change.

Take Sally Quinn, the novelist. She had a goal. When she graduated from Smith College, she wanted to be a movie star. And what did she do? "I did public relations for a pet festival in Coney Island. I was a Kelly Girl. I worked in Germany as a translator for Mercedes Benz. I worked at the Smithsonian Institution in Washington. I worked for Senator Barry Goldwater and then I worked for Bobby Kennedy on his campaign. I was social secretary for the Algerian Ambassador. I was a reporter for *The Washington Post.*" After four years at *The Washington Post,* she went to CBS as the first network TV anchorwoman on the morning news. "A disaster," she says, but "I wrote a book about the experience, which was a best-seller." And when she wrote her best-selling novel, she had a wealth of experiences to draw upon.

But what if you have done the Goal Analysis and you feel that it does not add up to anything very conclusive? This is possible, especially if you have not been working long. Many successful women had no idea about what they wanted when they started out. Barbara Walters was one. "When I was in college," Barbara told me, "it bothered me terribly that everyone seemed to know what she wanted to do. And I didn't. If I have any message to give to young women who are in college or in their first years of working, it is *Don't try to figure everything out.* You don't have to know what the rest of your life is going to be.

"Yes, you can have goals, but you don't have to know exactly what that job is going to be. Do what you love to do. And if you love to do it, you'll do it well and then you'll be successful."

Sherry Lansing, the film producer and former President of Production at Twentieth Century–Fox, also warns against becoming overly goal-oriented. "It seems to me when I talk to young women who want advice, they are always so goal-oriented that they never enjoy the process of what they are doing at the time. They are always looking to be chairman of the board while they are secretaries.

"My advice is, Enjoy the process of what you are doing at the moment. The results will come. If you are a reader, as I was a reader at the studio when I was earning the lowest salary, don't say, "Oh God, I hate this job. I can't wait to get out of it." Do your best. I thought reading was a great job. I became a real good reader. Then I became head of all the readers. I don't want to sound simplistic, but if you have a job and you hate it and you're just using everything as a stepping-stone, you are also missing life. Because this is your life. This very day. There is something wrong with not enjoying and respecting what you are doing and trying to be very good at it."

What these three women are saying is

Put yourself first.
Do what you want to do.
Do what makes you happy.

It worked for them. It will work for you. And just to keep in touch with yourself, I suggest that you schedule a Goal Analysis every six months, just the way you make an appointment to have your teeth cleaned. You will probably find that your goals and values keep changing. Your analyses will help you make the choices that will bring you closer to your new goals.

Six

EVEN WHEN you know what you want out of life, you may not get it. Love intervenes. Duty intervenes. Fate intervenes. At times all of us—male and female—choose to give up something that is important to us. What is important is that you make these choices with a full understanding of what they mean to you.

Let me give you two examples:

You give up a weekend ski trip with your husband because when you get home from work Friday you find seven-year-old Jessica in bed with a temperature of 103 and a raw, scratchy throat.

You lose a longed-for opportunity to be alone together with your husband, a chance for fun and a change of scene. But there are trade-offs.

There is peace of mind. You are right there at Jessica's bedside, taking her temperature, spooning chicken soup into her and reading *Mary Poppins* instead of hanging on the telephone at the ski lodge for the latest report from the sitter, instead of waking up at three in the morning full of worry and guilt, instead of deciding to cut the weekend short and heading home Sunday at dawn.

You also feel good that Jessica knows she means more to you than any ski weekend and that you are there when she needs you.

You have given up something, but the trade-offs are worth it. You end up feeling good about yourself. And a ski weekend can always be rescheduled. This is a minor decision, the nitty-gritty of everyday life.

The second situation involves major decisions. Your husband is transferred halfway across the country just when you have been promoted to manager of the mid-Atlantic division. Having to resign just when you have made an important career advance is a blow. You are giving up a lot. But you don't have to think twice. Of course you are going with him. Your husband and your marriage mean more to you than anything else in the world.

Is there a trade-off here? Yes, two of them. To start with, you are putting yourself first in terms of doing what you want most: to be with your husband and part of his life. And second, in terms of the bookkeeping of marriage, he owes you one. A big one. Someday when there is something you really want, something major—well, he owes you.

My husband and I do a lot of this kind of marital balancing of the books. For instance, I know Milt hates going to business dinners with me so I rarely ask him, but last winter I was invited to a dinner at the New Zealand Embassy in Washington and I didn't want to go alone. I asked Milt to go with me and he said, "Sure, if you want me to." But he got his trade-off.

When he gave a party a few weeks later for his office nurse who had been with him for twenty years, I flew back to New York from the West Coast just for the party. Normally I would have explained to her that I had to be in Los Angeles and I would have given her an extra-special present in gratitude for all she has done for Milt. She would have understood.

But I owed Milt one for that embassy dinner party, so I flew in for the party, and four hours later I flew back to Los Angeles to finish my commitments. I staggered around almost blind with fatigue the next day, but I managed.

Your choice in the hypothetical transfer situation may not be as simple as putting your husband and marriage ahead of your career. You love your husband dearly, but—

If you are going to regret the move forever after . . .

If you are going to resent him for making you do it . . .

If you feel it will abort your upward career climb . . .

If you are making the move in a spirit of martyrdom . . .

If one or more of these conditions prevail, don't do it. I am not saying: Break up your marriage. I am saying: Don't move. Not now. Negotiate. Look for alternatives.

A commuter marriage, for instance, may solve your problem on a temporary basis. I don't trust commuter marriages for reasons I explain in Chapter Thirteen, but if the arrangement is for a limited period of no more than six months, it could be the solution.

Any transfer is an iffy situation. Your husband may find that it was not what he expected or wanted. He may not fit into the new situation. He may be fired (this frequently happens in transfers). In any of these cases, if you have stayed behind and still have your job, he can come back home. He will be able to reestablish himself more easily in a familiar environment. One of you will still be doing well, instead of the two of you being fish out of water—and out of work.

If the new position turns out to be just what he wanted, six months should give you time to be sure of what *you* really want. You may be less reluctant to make the move after finding out how empty your life is without your husband.

You also will have had time to put out job feelers, and have reason to be optimistic about your career future in the new location.

On the other hand, you may discover that in the months you and your husband have been living apart during the week, your career has taken off, possibly because you have had more time and energy to invest in it. You may find your work more engrossing, more rewarding. You may wake up one morning and realize that your marriage is definitely in second place.

Then it is up to you to make your choice. What do you want most? Suppose you want to stay where you are and pursue your career. You find the commuter marriage comfortable, preferable to pulling up stakes and moving.

You tell your husband this. He may have been thinking along similar lines. Or he may have met someone who has become important in his life, more important than you. Commuter marriages have built-in perils. One five-year study of 121 such marriages revealed that a third of the men and women involved had had love affairs on the side. Or, it might be that your husband is deeply shaken by what you tell him and offers to move back and look for another job at home so the two of you can be together.

If you have children, a whole new dimension of decision-making is involved. In any case, you are faced with dozens of possible choices—none of them perfect.

It can be a turbulent and hurtful period; but what will hurt most is if you decide against yourself. You cannot retreat into a 1950s dependency on a husband-daddy who knows best. It is not true any longer—if it ever was—that whatever is best for him is best for you. The decision is yours.

How can you tell what the right choice is? You can't. There are no guarantees in life. All you can do is be very sure about what is most important to you. You must be equally sure that whatever choice you make will take you closer to your goal. No matter what you choose, you will be giving up something. Is the trade-off worth it?

Do not think of yourself as a monster of selfishness if in this hypothetical case, you do not make the traditional decision and follow your husband to a new city. Selfish or unselfish has nothing to do with it. Do a little role reversal and you will see what I mean. How many men would give up their slot on the fast track because their wife has been transferred 2,000 miles away? Some men would. No doubt about it. But not enough to make a dent in the statistics. Men's decisions tend to be self-regarding. The weight of history is on their side. Men have always expected their women to pack up and follow them.

Women cannot afford to be dependent if they want to make the most of themselves and their abilities. They must make choices. And the choices women face these days are far more difficult and far more basic than the choices men are called upon to make, as I explain in the next chapter.

SEVEN

"ONE HAS to make choices," says journalist Linda Grant. "It is just an unfortunate fact of being female. I don't think men have to make as many choices and as important choices as I did."

Marriage and children are no longer a woman's birthright. For more and more women, they are a matter of weighing priorities and possibilities. Close to 60 percent of married women find that a career or paid work outside the home is no longer an option, but a necessity. Current economic and social changes have put the security of financially comfortable stay-home wives at such risk that they must make unprecedented decisions about their lives.

MARRIAGE

Men take it for granted that they will get married. And so do most women. Men's big decision is *which* woman to marry.

But ambitious women, women who want to succeed in their chosen fields, must first decide if they *should* marry. And when. After that they can turn their attention to the choice of their future husband. As often as not, their decision (often made unconsciously) is to rule out marriage, as evidenced by a survey of top management in Fortune 1000 companies which showed that 52 percent of the women executives were unmarried, while 96 percent of the male executives were married.

Some women start out believing that of course they will eventually get married and have a family, but as the years go by they discover that they do not want to make the necessary concessions.

"If you had asked me twenty years ago, I probably would have told you that I wanted marriage and children," says Claire Heiss, manufacturing manager of simulations and controls for General Electric in Daytona, Florida.

"My values have changed. Today I do not want to get married. My work interferes with serious relationships. And when I do have a relationship, I am constantly being challenged to make all the trade-offs. I don't like that."

Other women want to marry, but not at the expense of their careers. Pat Collins, former arts and entertainment editor on the *CBS Morning News* and now head of her own company developing television shows, made a firm decision to postpone marriage until her career was well established.

"I noticed what happened to women who started out in television about the same time I did and who married. Some of them could not advance in their careers because their husband's career ruled out moving to another city. Others went ahead and moved, and in a short time their marriages dissolved.

"I moved a lot going from job to job, hoping to get one rung up on the ladder each time. It didn't seem to make sense to get serious about a man until I had reached the point in my career where I wouldn't have to move again. As far as I was concerned, that point was New York. If I met anyone

I liked, I would put him out of my mind. I couldn't ask him to give up what he was doing to move to New York if I did.

"By the time I met Joe, I was in New York and my career was going in the direction I wanted. I could entertain the idea of being serious about the right person."

Then there are women who have tried marriage and decided that while it may be a fine institution, it is not for them. Publisher Carole Sinclair, who has been married three times (twice to the same man), says, "I tried it and it didn't work. I worked as hard as I could at my marriages and they just didn't work.

"I've never found husbands to be particularly wonderful things to have. Male friends, lovers, companions, trusted confidants are terribly important, but husbands are not necessarily any of those things. There is a lot to be said for being held in the middle of the night, but there is nothing to be said for being held by the wrong person.

"I no longer want to be somebody's wife. I find that to get what I require in a man—companionship, intellectual diversion, love, sex, friendship—I have to piece it together with a couple of people. I suppose I could find someone who gave me all of these. But just assume that I did. The fact is that I am not willing to give them back what I want from them. If I have a problem, that's it."

Few women are willing to be as frank as Carole Sinclair, but many successful women share her feelings. Men do not give them what they feel they need. And they are so career-pressured that they are not able to return the time and tenderness and empathy that they want from a man.

Some women do not actually make their choice until they are confronted with a need to decide. And they are often surprised by the choice they make.

"I definitely put my job ahead of marriage," reports an executive in a utilities firm who asked to remain anonymous. "I thought I wanted to get married, but when marriage became a real possibility, I didn't want it."

She had had a long-term relationship which ended when

her lover started talking marriage. "Suddenly I realized that if I were to marry him, I would be faced with a whole new set of obligations that I wouldn't be able to meet while doing my job the way I want to do it. Sometimes I wonder if I made the right decision, but I always end up deciding that I did. My style is to go all-out on whatever I do. I don't see how you can go all-out on both a marriage and a career."

Marriage does not confront men with such choices. A wife is a career boost. Employers see a young man with a wife as responsible, ready to settle down, work hard and get ahead. They see a young woman with a husband as someone who is liable to get pregnant and stop working, no matter how much she may protest that she is as intent on getting ahead as any man in the organization. Or they believe that they will lose her if her husband is transferred to another area. Or, if she has children, they believe that she will always be running home to cope with domestic emergencies.

For men, wives are useful. They provide a home base, a pit stop in the rat race. Surveys show that the working wife—willingly or resentfully—usually assumes the same domestic responsibilities as the stay-home wife in addition to her job.

For women, a husband tends to mean more work. The man who believes that he should share domestic chores equally with his working wife is as rare as a black swan.

Let me say here, once and for all, that I am dealing in generalities. There are fantastic husbands out there, as caring and sharing as any woman. Business executive Mary Cunningham is married to one. "Bill and I share household responsibilities equally," she says.

"That word 'equally' is dangerous, because it gets into 'How many times did you empty the dishwasher?' or 'How many minutes of the day did you spend on housework?' I would say that we share equally, inasmuch as I never have the feeling that it is my job, not his, to do something of a domestic nature around the house. I don't find myself thanking him for helping me. We both assume it is our responsibility.

"Because of our work and client demands, in any given

week Bill could be doing eighty percent around the house and I would be doing twenty percent and it could be the other way around the next week. Bill is pleased to have a wife who wants to be his equal both in the home and professionally. He knows that you cannot be an equal professionally if you don't get some help at home. So we are partners in both situations."

Men like Bill Agee, Mary's husband, are the minority. I don't happen to be married to one. Milt is wonderful. I love him dearly and I cannot conceive of life without him; but if I come home to a hot meal after a ten-hour day in the television studio, it is because I have a casserole in the fridge ready to pop in the microwave.

CHILDREN

The big decision the working woman has to make is whether or not to have a child. Or two. Or more. Your hormones and your husband and your mother and your mother-in-law and heaven knows who else are usually on the side of motherhood. But the decision should be yours. It is your life. The decision to have a child is one of life's watershed decisions. Your life will never be the same again.

"I would like to have more children, but we won't," says Jacqueline Leo, cofounder and editor-in-chief of *Child* magazine. She and her husband have one daughter. He also has two children from his first marriage, but Jacqueline says this had nothing to do with their joint decision to have only one child.

"You can't do everything," she says. "I'm doing more than most and I'm very grateful to have the opportunity to do it. John and I planned for one child. Saved for one child."

Linda Grant made a different choice. "My first husband was fifteen years older than I," she said, "and he had two children from his first marriage. He was a foreign correspondent for a newsmagazine. I free-lanced and later worked for *Fortune* magazine. We traveled all the time.

"I decided not to have children. I didn't consider that a penalty. I really wasn't interested. First of all, in a two-journalist marriage you don't have a lot of money. It would have been very costly to have a child and full-time help and all that. I didn't see how it could be done. I also felt if I was going to have a journalism career and be taken seriously in that world of men, I couldn't be running home to a sick child or whatever.

"I have no regrets. I had a wonderful career. Saw the world. Interviewed many important people. If I'd had children, I would have missed all that."

But then, at forty-three and married to her second husband, Linda did have a baby. "It was a close call. I almost didn't have kids because I was working—and certainly had only one child because I was working."

The biological clock has a lot to do with the smaller family of the working woman. She puts off having children until her career is established. Biology then limits her to one or two children. As Linda says, "I was lucky to have a child at forty-three."

Other women who once put a high priority on having children find that fresh perceptions of reality keep their family size down. "When I was young and naive, I thought in terms of six children," says Karol Emmerich, who is very content with one child. "I have learned that I don't need six children to be fulfilled. One is so wonderful and so much fun that I could spend all my time with him."

Some women limit their families because they are aware of their own emotional limitations. Publisher Carole Sinclair has one child. "I wanted a child," she says, "but I don't wish I had another one. I can't stand the bickering and fighting that goes on when there is more than one child."

Barbara Walters warns against having children for the wrong reasons. "One thing you must think about when you're thinking about having children," she says, "is what it is going to be like the day they get out of the feet pajamas, the day they are no longer adorable. It is tough. If you just want a wonderful little creature to love, you can get a puppy.

"I've talked with women who know their biological clock is running down and think they should have a child before it is too late. I'll ask them why they want a child, and they say, 'I'm afraid I'll regret it when I'm in my fifties and sixties if I don't.'

"And I tell them, 'You won't regret it then. Have a child because you really want a child, not because somewhere down the line in twenty years or so, you may regret not having one.'

"In the final analysis, you have to do what your gut says is right. Trust your own instincts and your own judgments. If you are ambitious, if you love your work, if you want a career, then don't hate yourself because you don't have five children."

CAREER

Man may work from sun to sun,
But woman's work is never done.

The old saying is truer than ever. Work is the one thing few women have any choice about. The single woman must work to support herself. She could, of course, get married and stop working, since theoretically a married woman has the choice of being a stay-home wife or of pursuing a career outside the home. But only theoretically. In practice the majority of women have little choice. More than 60 percent of married women work outside the home. In 1986, nearly 63 percent of women with children under eighteen worked outside the home.

Many married women work because they want to—for the challenge, the stimulation. Because their work fascinates them. But most work because they must. "Their families need the

money," says Professor Dowell Myers of the University of
Wisconsin Business School. "They're not in a career. They're
in it because they need the bucks." It takes two salaries these
days for most families to maintain a middle-class standard of
living. A 1986 survey of 2,500 people revealed that most of the
men who participated counted on their wives' working. If
they had to support their families on their own salaries, the
men reported, they would have trouble meeting basic obligations like mortgage payments and food and medical bills.
The two-income family has become standard over the last
decade or so. "The next step," warns political-science professor Ethel Keline of Columbia University, "will probably
be the three-income family, with the husband having to take
a second job in order to keep up."

I am wholeheartedly in favor of women working. Every
woman should be able to support herself and her children
if need be. It is not that I am against women's staying home
and filling the roles of wife and mother just as their mothers
and grandmothers did, but the world has changed. Marriage
has changed, and a woman who cannot earn her own living
puts herself at risk.

When I was researching my last book, *What Every Woman
Ought to Know About Love and Marriage,* I learned that there
were 7.3 million more marriageable women than men in this
country. This means that many women will never marry. It
also means that many women who are married will not stay
married. At the time, I wrote that we had entered the era of
the disposable wife. We are still there.

The law of supply and demand applies to people as well
as to commodities. Women are less prized today than in generations past. Your husband may swear that he adores and
respects you and pledge eternal fidelity, but take a look at
the divorce rate. Almost every other marriage today ends in
divorce. Your marriage may be among the 50 percent that
will survive happily ever after—but how do you know?

"My niece got a divorce after twenty-two years of marriage," Julia Child reports. "She found out that her husband had had a mistress for eight years. Here she was spending all of her time on the house and the children and being a nice wife, and then—blooey! Now she's about forty-five and has no career. It's important for women to be able to take care of themselves because who knows what's going to happen?"

The ex-wife's standard of living falls 73 percent on the average after the divorce, while her ex-husband's increases 42 percent. "For women, divorce can be the gateway to destitution," writes Barbara Ehrenreich, a fellow at the Institute for Policy Studies in Washington, D.C. "For men, it is more likely to be a golden parachute to freedom."

It is not only divorce that puts a woman at risk, but illness, financial setbacks, accidents, death. Your ability to earn a living will not prevent disaster, but it will enable you to keep on going, to pay the mortgage, to make the car payments, to buy the groceries and to be in charge of your life.

"It is important to me to know that if I were suddenly alone, I could manage," says Gillian Sorensen. "Every woman should be able to do that. From the beginning, a woman should look at how she is leading her life and imagine that if tomorrow she were by herself, what it would be like. How would she support herself? And then take steps today to move toward being able to do that. It is not that you are necessarily going to have to support yourself, but it is important to have the inner feeling that you could."

Ordinary, garden-variety prudence dictates that a woman make herself capable of being self-supporting, but there is another and happier reason for a woman to work. It is good for you.

Studies indicate that the working wife is happier and healthier than the stay-home wife. She is more in charge of her life. Stronger. More interesting. She has more of a chance to develop her abilities. She experiences the joys of self-actualization.

But what has this to do with making choices? I am saying

that every woman must be able to make herself financially independent. There is no choice here. But there are choices in how you do it. I am not advocating that every woman juggle a full-time job and a family unless that is what she really wants to do. You can choose how you want to acquire the work skills and experience that will enable you to be financially independent if necessary.

Some women would never consider not working. Jacqueline Leo is one of them. "I was born to work," she says. "I was working when I was sixteen years old, going to college at night. That's what my life has always been about. I can't remember not having my own money that I earned myself. I was back at work four weeks after Alexandra was born, although that was because of a Dark Ages company policy. It was not my own choice."

Other women have established themselves in their careers before starting their families. Linda Grant's son was three months old when her employer, the *Los Angeles Times,* offered her a promotion from New York Financial Bureau chief to business editor—which meant leaving New York and moving to Los Angeles.

"I considered that job for about ten days," she says, "and finally turned it down because I felt I wouldn't have enough time with my child. That was probably the single biggest trade-off I've made in my career.

"I'm very happy, but I've reached a point now where I'd like a little less child and a little more work in my life, although I'm not champing at the bit.

"My son starts going to school five mornings a week this year, and I think this is going to be a period of reevaluation for me. I have editors calling me every couple of months asking when I want to come back to work. It's one of the good things about having waited as long as I did to have a child. I have been able to have these years at home with my son knowing that I can always pick up the phone and go to work tomorrow."

Chris Boe Voran, a corporation lawyer, also gave up her career to stay home and start her family.

"I could not envisage how I could possibly have a family life including children and keep my job," she says. "The job I had was making deals. I would get involved in a project and be working eighteen hours a day for two or three weeks at a time. We wanted children, but I wasn't getting pregnant, and I was concerned that working that hard and being that tired was affecting my ability to get pregnant.

"Another factor was I really wanted a home. I wanted to be able to invite people over. I wanted to be able to have food in the refrigerator. I wanted to read books, go to museums, take music lessons, meet my neighbors, do some gardening. I didn't want to be sixty-five and say, 'Damn it, I've never learned to play the piano. I never saw my child grow up.'

"I wouldn't call giving up my career a sacrifice, but there are things I miss. There is an explicit mechanism by which you know you are successful. People shake your hand and say, 'Hey, that was really good.' You read about your deals in *The Wall Street Journal*. You don't get that kind of feedback after a day at home.

"I'm happy that I did things in the order that I did, that I had my career first and then my family. I'm more relaxed and comfortable being home and raising my children because I had the satisfaction of being this sort of wild and crazy career girl.

"I have friends who are just now finishing raising their children and at forty are trying to start a career. A lot of them have spent the last five or ten years thinking, 'I wish I could be rich and famous and smart and powerful and successful, and I can't. I've missed it.' It's harder for a forty-year-old woman to go to work and really work hard than it is for a woman of twenty-five."

Chris, who lives in Los Angeles now, is relaxed about her future. "I think I will go back to work sometime," she says. "I don't know when. Maybe when my children go to school.

The problem is—after years of working on Wall Street, will everything else seem second-best? If I do something where the hours are shorter, where it's more mundane work, where you're the guy in the background doing the research or the nitty-gritty paper drafting, it's likely I'll be saying, 'God, this job is so worthless! Surely I'm capable of something better.'

"I don't know if my ego will take doing anything less than I used to do. It makes sense for me to take a nonpressured job and leave it at the office and not get so involved, but it's foolishness to believe that I would work any differently than I did before. I think I'm going to have to mellow out a lot before I go back to work."

Many women do manage to start their careers at forty and become notably successful. "My sister did it just the opposite from me," Linda Grant says. "She had her children in her early twenties and now she is an architect and loving her work, while I had my career first and now I'm loving being a mother for a few years."

My own sister took the same path. Elaine stayed home until all her children were in school and then she took herself off to law school. She went nights so that she could be home for the children during the day. If a child was ill, it did not present a crisis. She was there during the day, and her husband could take over in the evening when she went off to class. It was a long, hard grind, but today she is enjoying her flourishing legal career.

Some women used volunteer activities while their children were small to prepare for future careers. Madeleine Kunin worked at a Vermont television station until the first of her four children was born in 1961. For most of the next decade, her energies were concentrated on her home and family and volunteer work. She was active in the League of Women Voters. She organized a protest by doctors' wives against certain stands of the Vermont Medical Association. She lobbied to get a flashing light put up at a railroad crossing.

"My evolution into a politician developed not in opposition

to my role as a mother," she says, "but rather as an extension of it."

In 1972, she was elected to the Vermont House of Representatives. In 1978, she was elected Lieutenant Governor. In 1984, she was elected Governor of Vermont.

And then there are women who never in this world planned to work after they got married. Clara Knight (not her name) was one of them. She had held a routine secretarial job before her marriage, but for over a quarter of a century she had devoted herself to her husband, their three children and their home in a Boston suburb. Then Ed had a frightening heart attack.

"Another episode like that," the doctor warned her, "and we could lose him. With luck and good management, we may have him around for years to come. You can't count on it, though."

"Once I recovered from the shock—and it was a terrible shock—I realized just how empty my life was going to be without Ed. I could not even see a life for myself. Rattling around in a big empty house, the children all off on their own, what was I going to do for the rest of my life? I was only fifty.

"I decided I had only one choice: go to work. I rented a typewriter and polished up my old skills. I took a word-processing course. And then when Ed was back on his feet and back at the office, I went looking for a job. I found one paying minimum wage in a nonprofit organization.

"Today I run an employment agency for older men and women who would rather work than stay home and collect Social Security. Last year I opened a branch in another Boston suburb, and I'm looking into the possibility of franchising.

"Ed is just fine these days," she says. "I don't want my name used because I don't want people to know just how close he came to death twelve years ago. He took early retirement at sixty and has been working in the agency with me ever since. It has been a wonderful time for both of us. "And if he ever does have a second heart attack, now I have something to fill my life. I'm no longer a helpless housewife. I've proved myself as a businesswoman."

Marriage, children, career. These are basic to women's lives. And so is the necessity of making choices about them today. The women who have shared their choices in these chapters knew what they wanted. They put themselves first. They are in charge of their lives. And they know that once you make a choice, it frees you. It frees you to act. It frees you from the stress of indecisiveness. It frees you to proceed with your life.

PART THREE

MARRIAGE

EIGHT

THE MAJOR problem faced by successful women is how to combine career and marriage. Marriage can be the most rewarding and exciting relationship of a woman's life. It can also be the most difficult.

The women I interviewed who have succeeded in forging a happy combination of marriage and career had a potent force on their side. Love. Without love, any marriage is hollow, liable to collapse at the first threat of a storm. Many men and women—especially in the early years of marriage—who believe they love their partners are actually in the throes of euphoric infatuation: a delightful state, but not one that can sustain a marriage. Love, real love, is not simply a state of bliss. It is an ever-changing state, the result of time and emotional development, of trust and commitment.

Some of the wisest words about love and marriage were written by psychiatrist and psychoanalyst Dr. Willard Gaylin. "Love is something beyond pleasure," he wrote in his book *The Discovery of Love*. "Love describes a state of existence, a tacit set of contracts, a moral arrangement, a changed sensibility, an altered identity. It is a process, not an event." To fuse one's fate with that of another in marriage demands both trust and commitment. "Trust is an act of faith. It is love's testament," Dr. Gaylin says. "Commitment, on the other hand, is an act of will and a statement of intent. It is a promissory note to love."

The dual-career marriage demands more trust and more commitment, perhaps, than a marriage in which only one partner works, since the pressures tend to be greater. There are more divorces among dual-career couples than among the rest of the married population. Destructive forces are constantly at work in a dual-career marriage. Unless you recognize them and deal with them, your marriage may be doomed. Most of these pressures seem to stem from lack of time.

"There is never enough time," says Gillian Sorensen, who is married and has a daughter. "What I need is an eight-day week. And I'd like to have the eighth day for myself."

Felice Schwartz says that she has been "racing time" all the forty-odd years of her marriage.

"What I want is time," says Karen Nussbaum, who lives in Cleveland with her husband and two small children. "I'd love to take a sabbatical for a few months. Just stay home. Do jigsaw puzzles. That kind of thing. Clear my mind and see what pops up as being important."

Marilyn Moore is married and has three children. When we interviewed her, she was finishing up her last week at the Madison (Wisconsin) Gas and Electric Company and getting ready to take up a new position as manager of records management at Frito-Lay in Dallas. "Time management is a problem," she said. "Trying to do all the things that I want to do is a problem. I'm always feeling guilty. If I stay late at work, well then—what about home? If I have to work on the weekends, I feel guilty. When I go to school functions and I see the children going through different stages—fifth grade, eighth grade, graduation—then I think about the years whizzing past. It makes me sad."

"It is like quicksand," an art restorer who requested anonymity said. "Every day I sink deeper and deeper into the world of the vacuum cleaner and supermarket and the nursery-school car pool. It is getting so that I feel guilty when I close the door behind me to go to my studio. And I *hate* that feeling. My work is important. I have two commissions from major museums in my studio right now. I'm desperate for time. But I love my husband. I love the twins. I guess this is the trade-off you make for love and marriage."

There is no magic formula for adding hours to the day and days to the week. When it comes to time, there is no absolutely satisfactory solution. The married woman who is serious about her career and her marriage will never have enough time. Never in this world.

The problem is, How do you live with a perennial shortage of time? I suggest you think of yourself as a pioneer on a brand-new frontier. Assess your priorities. Make your choices. Do the best you can.

The woman who loves her husband, who has trust in him and in her marriage, who is committed to him and her marriage will find that love is her most effective tool in negotiating solutions to the problem of never enough time as well as all the other problems that inevitably arise in marriage.

In the following chapters I will tell you how some successful women have coped with time problems in their marriages. Successful women are no different from other working women in that all of us face the same problems. Their ways of coping may help you handle similar problems.

I will also give you some psychological tools that can be helpful. But the love you need to work out stresses in your marriage—that I cannot give you. That has to be your own contribution to your special blend of marriage and career.

NINE

THE BLOCKBUSTER trade-off most women make when they choose to combine career and marriage is time. Woman after woman told me that there was never enough time. Not enough time for their husbands. For their children. For their work. Not enough time for sex, for friendship, for fun. Not enough time for this and that and the other.

I can't remember one day myself in the last twenty-five years when I did not feel I had too much to do. My daughter calls me the Queen of Busy. I am forever trying to do several things at once. I feel like a juggler who is constantly handed one more ball to keep in the air. And yet I love it—most of the time.

Too often the trade-off turns out to be abysmally unfair. Single women may feel harried by time pressures, but it is the working wife who is really under siege. For the working woman, marriage tends to be like a second job. She just moves from one workplace to another, exchanging the demands of her career for the demands of her husband, children and home. One study of 216 executives—half men, half women—revealed that the women viewed their home life as a burden, another major responsibility. Men see their homes as a refuge, a place to get away from it all.

The feminist ideal was that husbands would share domestic chores equally with their working wives; but statistics show that the average working wife spends twenty-five hours a week on household tasks, while her husband spends only twelve. A recent study reported in the *Journal of Marriage and the Family* found that the more money a wife makes, the more housework her husband does. Money is power, no doubt about it, but the increments of work done by a man around the house increase so slightly, on the average, that they are practically infinitesimal. I would not want you to count on your husband's starting to do more housework after you get your next raise. I make significantly more money than my husband makes in his medical practice—and I do significantly more work around the house. And by no means am I an exception.

Too often the working wife finds herself cooking dinner while her husband relaxes in front of the television set. Too often she finds herself too tired for sex by the time the children are finally in bed. Too often her resentment of the unequal work load coupled with the stress of running a household and pursuing a career results in pernicious fallout on a marriage.

Many women believe that if their husbands would only share the housework and other domestic responsibilities equally, the time problem would be solved. They are wrong.

Time is not the real problem. When time becomes a major issue in a dual-career marriage, it is usually a mask for the real force that tears too many of these marriages apart—the power struggle. This struggle can pervade and weaken the whole fabric of a marriage. It can ruin your sex life and turn your finances into a major battleground. And in some instances, there is absolutely no way to resolve the struggle.

This was the case with Ida Roberts, vice president for cor-

porate communications at the SE Bank Corporation in Miami.
"My husband tried to make me into the perfect homemaker and mother," Ida said. "He did not mind that I worked,
as long as I did everything else perfectly. He never shared
any of the household responsibilities. He said those were
woman's work. Woman's work to do the laundry. Woman's
work to take care of the children. Woman's work to do the
cooking. Woman's work to keep the house immaculate. I tried
to get him to help, but he said no and that was it. He never
changed a diaper or fed a bottle to a baby in his life."

After two children and fifteen years of marriage, Ida got
a divorce. There was nothing left of the relationship. No
tenderness. No love. And as for sex, "You can't have a sexual
relationship when you are at war," she pointed out.

"It was a problem of a poor choice on my part," she says
now, "an inability to recognize what real strength is. The man
I am seeing now wants to share any responsibilities we might
have in the future. I would advise women to be careful about
the type of man they marry. Instead of looking for someone
very dominant and powerful, they should look for a man
who is willing to do his share."

Ida Roberts is representative of more working wives than
you might believe. When *Woman's Day* magazine surveyed
3,009 of its readers, it came up with some surprises. Only
half of the women would marry their present husbands if
they had it to do again. Sixty-three percent said that their
husbands rarely helped around the house. Fifty-five percent
of the women surveyed worked outside the home. Their
median age was forty-one.

In most marriages, the power struggle first erupts around
the issue of housework. Many men feel that every time they
mop the kitchen floor or clean a toilet, they have lost power
and status and their wife has gained power and status. And
she has—simply because she did not have to mop that floor
or clean that toilet.

The working wife who sees her husband reading the paper
or working on a business report while she cleans up the

kitchen after dinner feels exploited and angry. She feels devalued. She would like time to work on her own business reports and read the paper. She works as hard at her job as he does at his—and here she is, a domestic slave.

Women today make up nearly 40 percent of the professional and executive labor force, compared with about 25 percent two decades ago. Most of these women are married. What this adds up to is a social revolution that is forging new roles for both men and women.

"Behind the facts and figures are men and women working out alternate life styles within the context of these changing societal patterns," report researchers Lucia Albino Gilbert, Ph.D., of the University of Texas, and Vicki Rachlin, Ph.D., of the State University of New York. "These individuals," they say, "are faced with a number of important adjustments as they attempt to integrate their occupational and family roles."

It is not going to be easy. Neither men nor women have readily available role models for their new lives. Today's dual-career couples are in the vanguard of problem-solvers as they search for ways to share the responsibilities of homemaking and child care as well as those of economic support. The traditional divisions of rights and responsibilities are no longer viable.

Some men are philosophically and actually committed to sharing. "We both do housework and yard work; we both cook; we both wash dishes," Anthony Brandt wrote in *Esquire*. "We discuss almost everything that needs to be done. We argue about how often the garbage should be taken to the dump, whether or not we should each do our own laundry . . . When we are done arguing, we negotiate. I'll do this if you do that. It is hard work.

"I have come to realize that we are two adults wrestling with each other and carrying a lot of history on our backs: the history of women's demands for equality, the history of this society's collective attempt to find new, fairer and more satisfying ways to be married. We have become a partnership with no junior member, each supporting the other, each making equal sacrifices for and commitments to the other."

Brandt belongs to the avant-garde. Few men look forward to coming home and cooking dinner or doing the wash. Their fathers never had to. And they don't want to. Even the most fair-minded of men will turn a blind eye to a sinkful of dishes or an unmade bed. In a study of 680 couples, Drs. Catherine Ross and John Mirowsky, sociologists at the Unversity of Illinois, found that among dual-career couples, the wives' "central problem is getting their husbands to share the housework."

What can a woman do?

The first thing she can and should do is to resolve that the issue of who is going to do what around the house and how much will not be allowed to poison her marriage. When we interviewed Dr. Terry Weill, a New York psychiatrist and mother of one, she pointed out that "household responsibilities are only a small part of the contract that any couple make with each other on how they are going to conduct their shared lives." I strongly suggest that a woman should tell herself that somehow or other she is going to work out the problem and put it behind her. Arguing over the division of household chores is not worth the physical and psychic energy one wastes on it. That energy should go into more rewarding areas of one's marriage.

The second thing a woman should do is let her husband know what she expects of him. He is not a mind reader. If you do not let him know that you expect him to share the work, chances are he will let you do it all.

"If I were to try to advise working wives," says Joan Rivers, "I'd say that your husbands have got to understand that you are working as hard as they are. When you get home at night, things have to be shared. They can't just flop down on the couch. You're as tired as they are.

"When you are working and you are working full time and you are working at a high-pressure job, you've just got to have a husband who understands that it drains you as much as his work drains him. And this goes for every area of your marriage."

Political scientist Jeane Kirkpatrick, former U.S. Ambassador to the United Nations, says, "A lot of it is making clear demands. At times when I thought that the distribution of work was unfair, I said so. And when I did, my husband helped and my sons helped—and some things we just left undone. I never felt resentful. Generally speaking, women who feel resentful about their husbands and children not helping don't demand that they do so."

Nancy Evans, president and publisher of the Doubleday publishing company, agrees with Ambassador Kirkpatrick. "One thing I've learned," she says, "is that you have really got to set ground rules right at the beginning. If you slip into bad habits, you will stay there. And if that bad habit is that you are doing all the work, the guy you are living with will gladly let you continue to do all the work. So I think you have to be conscious of it and establish good patterns from day one."

There are all kinds of communication, as Heloise, my fellow columnist in *Good Housekeeping*, points out.

For women who are having trouble getting their husbands to do anything, she says, "I know that the approved thing to do is say, 'Let's sit down and talk about it' and then the two of you talk and you draw up a chart of who does what and that's that. That may work for some families, but a lot of the time it doesn't.

"If it doesn't, you can do what several women have written me they did. The funniest letter was from a woman who said she had talked to her husband and talked and talked and he still dropped his underwear and towels on the floor the way he had done all their married life. She finally said, 'Look, no longer. I work too.' And she picked up a hammer and some nails and nailed everything he dropped to the floor. I don't know what that did for their relationship, but it alleviated her frustration.

"I think sometimes the only thing you can do is say, 'Hey

look, I can't do it all. Plus it's unfair.' And then stop doing it all. It may take a month of having the kitchen a mess, wet towels on the bathroom floor and his underwear all over the bedroom floor, but hopefully he will get the message and shape up. When I was a child, my mother complained and complained about my messy room. Finally she said, 'I'm not going to let myself be aggravated by this any longer.' And she just shut the door to my bedroom. After a while I couldn't stand it myself. And I cleaned it up."

A lot of the flak and bitterness over this subject comes from poor communications, unvoiced expectations. If you feel that you are doing more than your fair share, you must speak up.

The fact is that it is quite possible for a woman to be married and have a career and run a household without driving herself crazy—and without any power struggles over who should empty the dishwasher. As proof, here is a baker's dozen of successful women, all with different lifestyles, all in different fields, who report that the sharing of household responsibilities presents no problem at all in their lives.

Barbara Walters told me, "Neither my husband nor I have too many household responsibilities, although I very much run the house. I supervise everything and know everything that happens. But I don't do any of the day-to-day work myself. And I can't remember the last time I was in a grocery store."

"We have a wonderful housekeeper and she does just about everything," says investment counselor Joyce Buchman, a vice president in the New York investment firm of Peter C. Cannel. "My husband has never helped around the house. And I don't do much either. I just don't see any virtue in housework, especially when you can afford to hire help."

Helen Gurley Brown, married to film producer David Brown, whose credits range from *The Sound of Music* to *Patton* to *Jaws*, says, "David never helps out. He would starve before he would get something to eat for himself. When I'm out of the city, he goes to restaurants for breakfast and lunch and we hope somebody takes him in for dinner.

"I used to take care of sending out his shirts and dry cleaning, but over the years he has become responsible for his own wardrobe. This is a good thing for women to remember. They may not be able to get the guy to cook or clean or mop or scrub or make beds, but they can make him responsible for his own clothes."

Psychiatrist Phyllis Harrison-Ross, professor of clinical psychology at New York Medical College and director of the Community Mental Health Center at Metropolitan Hospital, says, "When I was in college, I lived in a co-op dorm where at different times I was cook and waitress and maid. One thing I learned is that if you have a list of what has to be done and you just go ahead and do it, it is done and over with.

"When I got married, my husband and I drew up a work schedule of things that had to be done daily, weekly, monthly and so on. Then we worked out a checkoff list that showed everything that had to be done and how often. And then," she says, "we hired someone to do the work."

"We both work eight and ten hours a day and we rely on our housekeeper for the practical aspects of life—laundry and dinner on the table. All that. I couldn't do it without her help," says Gillian Sorensen, who is married to Theodore Sorensen, an attorney and writer who was special counsel to President John F. Kennedy. "On weekends when the housekeeper is away, I do the cooking and he does the washing up."

Jeane Kirkpatrick says, "My husband is not terribly helpful around the house. He never has been, but this has never been an issue. We have always had household help. I stayed home for nine years to take care of our sons (I had three boys under four years of age at one point), but I never considered for one minute that I was staying home to take care of the house. One of my great goals during those nine years was to make enough money doing free-lance work to hire household help."

Julia Child, the cook and author, says, "My husband and I have always worked together. If we are having a dinner party, he always sets the table. If I'm pressed for time, he will snap the beans or something like that. We have a cleaning woman who comes in four hours once a week when we are in California. And in Cambridge, where we have a great big house, we have a professional cleaning service. But housework has never been an issue with us. Real companionship with one's husband makes all the difference."

Julie Eisenhower, author and editor and mother of three, says, "In some marriages I think the husbands are a little more involved in the home, but David really is not very involved. I have realized that for some eighteen years now, so I just deal with it by understanding that this is the way it is going to be.

"You know, if you really like the person and they have the other great qualities and are easy to live with, then you just don't want to make an issue of it. And there is nothing I have a burning desire to do that is more important to me than having a family and a happy marriage."

Dividing up household responsibilities came naturally to columnist Heloise and her husband. "What we worked out is that I really don't like to do yard work. There are a lot of people who enjoy gardening and mowing and trimming. I don't. So David does all that, and he does a wonderful job. He doesn't care about the kitchen, so I do that.

"I think there is a new era dawning, though. Knock on wood. One day this may no longer be a problem for any woman. Women have been teaching their sons how to do laundry and how to cook and how to clean. I get this in letters to my column all the time. Now, whether these boys are going to do it when they get married is a different matter. Let us hope that with the new generation coming up, husbands will say, 'Hey, I know how to do this' and not feel it is unmasculine to do the laundry or whatever."

When I asked Jane Kennedy, sportscaster, television personality, president of her own production company and mother of one-year-old Savannah, if her husband, actor and entrepreneur Bill Overton, shared household responsiblities equally, her answer was "Absolutely!"

"We both have our offices in the same office building, so we spend a lot of time together during the day. That way he gets to see the baby a lot, because I take her with me. We drive home together, and when we get in, I usually take Savannah up and start changing her and freshening her up and he will take care of whatever needs to be unpacked out of the car. Then when I start getting dinner ready, he takes care of Savannah and of setting the table. As soon as she eats, I take her upstairs for her bath and he clears the table and does the dishes. Everything just seems to work out naturally."

Karen Nussbaum and her husband have no household help at all. "We were very conscious of wanting to share household and child responsibilities," she said. "For a long time we tried to divide everything fifty–fifty, but we found that it actually works out better if each does the kind of thing he or she likes. For instance, my husband does most of the laundry and I do the cooking. He cleans the house better than I do. I keep it stocked better."

Karol Emmerich has a housekeeper come in one day a week. "Otherwise," she said, "we divide household responsibilities sort of inside–outside. He takes care of the yard. I supervise the house. We each take care of our own dry cleaning.

"I pay the bills. From my husband's perspective, this is a boring, unpleasant task. From my perspective, it's one I like. I always want to know where we stand."

"On household responsibilities, the truth is that I lucked out," says Nancy Evans. "My husband does more than half the work. He cooks and I don't. He is much better at things

like remembering to get milk. I would never think to pick
up milk on the way home. I think he would be thrilled,
though, if I cooked even one meal a week. Every year I
resolve that I *will* cook one meal a week, but so far it hasn't
happened.

"I don't like housework either, although I like having the
house orderly and pretty. I'm the one who brings flowers
home. And one thing I do love is polishing the silver. What
we do is have a woman come in twice a week to clean and
pick up. The rest of the time the bed is lucky if it gets made."

It seems so easy, doesn't it?

Well, these are the ideal situations. This is how it can be
for a working wife if there is enough money to hire household
help. And this is how it can be if her husband is sweetly
reasonable and egalitarian-minded.

But what if there isn't?

And what if he isn't?

What if you have a husband like mine?

Ah, that is another story altogether.

What I have is a husband who would not push a vacuum
cleaner if the floor were knee-deep in dust or start dinner
before I got home at night no matter how hungry he was.
What I have is a husband who has yet to learn—after sixteen
years—where in our apartment house the laundry room is.
What I have is a husband who refuses to have full-time help,
although we can easily afford it, because he does not want
anyone around the house when he is home except his wife—
and on occasion his daughter and her family.

This refusal to have any outsider around the house dates
way back to when we were first married in the 1950s. We
were poorer than the proverbial church mice. We lived with
my folks for the first three years of our marriage while Milt
was going to medical school and I was working for my doc-

torate in psychology. We had my childhood bedroom, two doors down the hall from my folks' room.

It was enormously easy in one way. We had no household tasks. We came home and sat down and ate our supper and then we studied. Emotionally, however, it was difficult. It seemed as if we were never alone.

Milt and I were not only adjusting to our new roles as husband and wife, he was also adjusting to living with my parents. He wanted to assume his traditional role as head of our little household, but as long as we lived with my folks, that was my father's role.

There were always little frictions. I was ill once and had been to several doctors who were unable to find out what was wrong (it finally turned out that I was allergic to monosodium glutamate). One night Dad said, "Why don't you go to Dr. So-and-So?"

"That's ridiculous," Milt, the medical student, objected. "What would he know that the other doctors didn't?"

I went anyway. I was so miserable I would have gone to a veterinarian if anyone had suggested it. As it turned out, Dr. So-and-So was no more help than the others. But when Milt learned that I had consulted him, he was furious that I had taken my father's advice over his.

In retrospect, he was right. I was still more daughter than wife. There were dozens of little episodes like this, none of them serious, but enough to make my husband determine that once we had our own place there was not going to be anyone around.

When we were finally on our own in our own little walk-up apartment, I added cleaning and cooking to my research and teaching jobs and we lived very happily. When Lisa was born, I stopped working for three years to take care of her. Milt loved those years. I had more time for him, and he was king of the castle; but I went crazy with boredom. I remember being more tired during those years than ever in my life. I didn't have anything to look forward to. The days were endless. I thrive on deadlines. And my only deadline was having dinner ready for Milt when he got home, which was hardly a challenge. When I take care of my grandchildren, whom I adore, I have the same enormous fatigue. I like playing with a child, but you can't do that all the time. And you shouldn't. They have to learn to play by themselves. And for me, sitting and watching a child play is torture after the first ten minutes.

My life changed when Lisa started nursery school and I began my lecturing and broadcasting career. It has been fast-paced and high-pressured ever since. Time has always been at a premium. But to this day, I make do with a woman who comes in mornings to clean and do the laundry. I have never complained, because I understand how Milt feels, and we manage very well. I enjoy cooking and running the house.

Over the years, however, Milt has changed from a man who never lifted a finger to one who has taken on a few self-selected duties. For instance, these days we do the weekly grocery shopping together. Milt now makes the coffee every morning and cooks breakfast every weekend, whether it is just the two of us or a houseful of family and guests. And he makes gorilla sandwiches.

I would say that our split of domestic responsibilities is 99 percent to 1 percent. And I do the 99. Is this fair? Of course not. Do I get upset about it? Not at all. I made my choice long ago. My husband and my marriage come first.

It is far more important to me that we spend what time we have together happily, not bickering over trivia like dusting and bed-making. For they truly are trivia when compared with the rest that life has to offer. If you weigh dust kittens under the bed against laughter and dirty dishes in the sink against good sex, laughter and sex, in my book, win out every time.

Actually, the house stays clean enough with my part-time help, although my interior decoration leaves much to be desired. We have the latest in television and recording equipment—in our bedroom. Milt has one of the world's best racing bicycles—garaged in the living room. We are still eating on the game tables we bought when we moved into our first apartment. We told ourselves that when we had enough money to buy a dining table, the game tables could be put to their proper use. But by the time we had enough money, I was too busy to go shopping for a dining table.

Someday I am going to get a pad to go under the living-room rug and mend the chair with the wobbly leg and get the sofa re-covered. And someday I hope to have time to buy outdoor furniture to put on our thirty-first-floor terrace with its magnificent view of the Hudson River. But I don't quite know when that day will come.

When the television crew came to film our apartment for *Life Styles of the Rich and Famous,* they looked around with shock and a certain amount of despair. I had warned them that we lived very modestly, but they had not expected it to be quite that modest. They ended up by moving most of our furniture to one end of the living room and doing the best they could.

Milt's willingness for me to pursue a career that sends me flying back and forth across the country every week and entails crazy hours, his pride in my accomplishments, mean more to me than any bit of housework that he could ever do. Nor is his commitment less to me than mine to him. He lives up to his vows to love, honor and cherish me. His intellectual and emotional support enriches my life. Our marriage is hardly egalitarian on the housework front, but it is absolutely egalitarian in support and respect and love. I have always cherished what he wrote about me in an introduction to one of my first books. "My wife has shown me that a happy wife makes for a happy marriage," he wrote. "Joyce has remained an individual and has sought her own direction in her professional life, as have I. In our marriage, however, our paths have been parallel. There has been nothing but love and a mutual desire for each other's success."

I am not a Mrs. Goody-Goody, a one-of-a-kind freak. Other successful women have the same attitude. "If someone looked at it from outside," says Gillian Sorensen, "they would say, 'You are doing more,' but I feel that in terms of Ted's encouragement and the interest that he always expresses in my work and my problems, I get full support. That makes up to me for any housework that might not be done."

Now, what happened to induce my husband to take on his handful of domestic chores? I take full credit for this development, and I tell you in the next chapter just how it came about.

TEN

How DID I get my husband to make the coffee at breakfast and take on the few other chores he does? Not by sweet reasoning, not by nagging, not by complaining that I had to do everything, not by demanding that he shoulder part of the burden, but by making use of simple psychological tools that anyone can use. The first and most important is Positive Reinforcement, which is a form of Operant Conditioning. It works best when combined with Intermittent Reinforcement.

By the end of this chapter, you will understand just how these tools work and be able to use them yourself. They can be useful in many areas of your life—not only with your husband, but with your children, your in-laws, your employer and coworkers, your employees, with almost anyone whose behavior you want to change.

POSITIVE REINFORCEMENT

Positive Reinforcement encourages wanted behavior. Negative Reinforcement is used to discourage unwanted behavior. Many people make the mistake of using Negative Reinforcement when they should be using Positive. All of us use Positive and Negative Reinforcement in our dealings with others, even though we may not be aware of the psychological terms for what we are doing.

Positive Reinforcement is hugging your husband when he does a load of laundry.

Negative Reinforcement is telling him he used too much detergent.

Positive Reinforcement is saying, "I can't believe it. All the Saturday chores are done and it's only noon. It really makes a difference when we all pitch in. What do you say we all go to the movies and have a pizza afterwards for supper? Or better still, what if we send the kids to the movies and we stay home and play Love in the Afternoon?"

Negative Reinforcement is saying, "You see, if you'd just do your share on Saturdays, we'd have time to visit my mother. She's always complaining that she never sees us." Hardly the kind of bait that is going to get him to do his share of the Saturday cleanup.

Silence can be a truly golden form of Positive Reinforcement at times. Joan Rivers says she and her late husband shared household responsibilities equally. "We didn't work it out or discuss it. It just evolved," she says. "When we first got married, Edgar said, 'I'm not going to do anything. The household is your responsibility.'

"But then the first night we were in our apartment, it was, 'Let me help you clear the table. . . . Hand me a dish towel. . . . Let me take the garbage out.'

"So I figured that if I just shut up, things would work out fine. And they did."

A wise woman, that Joan. If she had said, "Hey, I thought you weren't going to do anything," that would have been

Negative Reinforcement. Edgar could have thought she was mocking him. He would probably have replied, "That's right," and dropped the dish towel.

Criticism is Negative Reinforcement. If your husband does not do something your way or as well as you do, bite your tongue. "Women tend to feel that everything has to be done their way," says psychologist Judith Kuriansky. "If the husband doesn't perform according to their standards, they start nagging. This gets you nowhere as far as help goes. It can also play havoc with a man's performance in bed. Few men feel good about sleeping with Mommy—and a pretty high-handed Mommy at that."

The wise woman will cultivate a blind eye and a tolerance for imperfection. "He doesn't see a lot of the things that bother me," says Chris Boe Voran, "like really wiping up the counter after you've cooked; but I just let it go." As Jacqueline Leo points out, "Men don't see the dirt. It's not in their genes."

"I have never been concerned about whether everything is picked up," admits Jeane Kirkpatrick. "My standards aren't very high. I'm nearsighted, and furthermore, I'm slightly absentminded about domestic things. A college-professor type."

"My feeling is that dust does not kill," says Mary Anne Devanna, coordinator of the Center for Career Research and Human Resource Management at the Columbia University Business School. "I leave the beds unmade sometimes, and I don't panic when someone arrives unexpectedly. I know women with Ph.D.s who feel compelled to spend fifty hours a week on housework. You have to decide what your standards are."

"I had to grit my teeth in the beginning when Irv started making the beds," says Felice Schwartz. "I could have made them in seconds. It took him twenty minutes.

"You have to guard against doing it all yourself just because you can do it better," she warns. "If you take over a chore your husband is doing simply because you can do it better and faster and it exasperates you to watch him, you have

simply trapped yourself into owning that chore." And you
have given him a large dose of Negative Reinforcement that
he can take advantage of by making such statements as, "What's
the use? According to you, I don't do anything right. You'll
be better off doing it yourself."

I know it is hard to refrain from criticizing. I know just
how irritating it can be to watch someone taking twice as long
as necessary to do a job—and doing it badly. But give him
time. If practice does not make perfect, at least it will make
better.

And when you feel you can't stand it one more minute
and are about to tell him what an absolutely rotten job he is
doing, here is something you should do instead.

Smile!

I am quite serious. A smile not only makes you look happier, it makes you feel happier. "When you smile, muscles
press on the veins in the face sending blood to the brain,"
says Dr. R. B. Zajonc, psychologist and director of the Research Center for Group Dynamics at the University of Michigan. This influx of blood to the brain, according to Dr.
Zajonc, triggers the release of neurotransmitters that make
you feel good. So when you cannot bottle up your criticisms
any longer, stop and smile. You will be happier for it.

When Johnny Mercer sang, "Accentuate the positive, elim-
inate the negative," he knew what he was singing about. As
my grandmother—and probably yours—used to say, "You
can catch more flies with honey than with vinegar."

And what do you use for honey?

Flattery is one of the most powerful forms of Positive Reinforcement. Effective flattery works two ways. First, it has
what psychologists call the Self-Enhancement Effect. Your
husband, for instance, likes to think well of himself. Like all
of us, he has doubts about himself from time to time, so when
you tell him something that makes him think well of himself,
it is welcome—and reassuring. Second, he likes you more
than ever for appreciating just how fine a person he is.

Studies of the ways flattery influences behavior and attitudes reveal that the compliments people like most, the ones they treasure and remember, tend to be about their personality and character. Next come compliments on their achievements.

A man will take a certain pleasure in being told that he is handsome. And he will enjoy hearing that you like his new sports jacket. But what really gives him those warm fuzzies is to be told what a superior person he is, what a sterling character.

If you tell him that you admire his sense of fairness or the way he always makes other people feel good about themselves or his ability to understand both sides of a question or his scrupulous insistence on doing his share, he will cherish it. He will think about it every now and then and it will make him feel good all over again.

You can compliment him on a job well done (or well done in his eyes). "That floor looks a hundred percent better. . . . This salad dressing is great. What did you put in it? . . . I had a shock when I opened the fridge. It's no longer a disaster area. I can't remember when it's looked that good."

Secondhand compliments can be particularly effective. For instance, "Louise told me she wished Josh was as good a host as you are. She was impressed by the way you introduced our new neighbors to everyone at the barbecue and made them feel at home."

OPERANT CONDITIONING

The theory behind Positive Reinforcement is that if a person is rewarded for doing something, he is likely to do it again so he will be rewarded again. It is one form of a method of changing behavior that is known as Operant Conditioning.

There is a laboratory experiment that most students studying clinical psychology have to perform at one time or another that illustrates just how this works.

A rat is placed in a cage, empty except for a metal bar.

The rat does what comes naturally. It explores the cage. At some point in its explorations, the rat hits the metal bar. This triggers a mechanism that allows a food pellet to fall into the cage. The rat increases its exploring activity around the area where it found the food. Sooner or later it hits the bar again and gets another food pellet. Before long, the rat has learned that pushing the bar has something to do with getting food. It starts pressing the bar to get more food. It is no longer sheer chance when the rat touches the bar.

Pressing a bar is not a normal response in a rat. In their natural state, rats do not go around pressing metal bars. This bar-pressing behavior is learned behavior.

You can teach people much the same way. They learn faster than rats, but they are just as interested in rewards. If a man knows that every time he cleans the bathroom or vacuums, sex is going to be great that night, he will scrub the tiles or vacuum the rugs more willingly. If he knows that if he helps you clean house, the two of you can get out on the golf course earlier on Saturdays, he will pitch in and help more readily.

But isn't all this Operant Conditioning and Positive Reinforcement manipulation? And isn't it wrong to manipulate your husband?

Yes, it is manipulaton. Wrong to manipulate your husband? It depends. If you are trying to make him believe something that is not so, that is wrong. But if you are trying to get him to do his fair share of work around the house, I consider this permissible. And it is certainly a far more agreeable kind of persuasion than nagging.

We are cultured to believe that manipulation is a twelve-letter dirty word, yet we all manipulate. Parents manipulate their children. When you want your three-year-old who is having a wonderful time in his rubber-ducky pool to come out because he is shivering, you don't say, "Come out of the water this instant. You're freezing to death." He would deny that he was cold and resist coming out. Instead you say, "It's time for juice and cookies. Which do you want, chocolate-chip or oatmeal?" And he comes running.

Lawyers manipulate. Bankers manipulate. Editorial writers. Religious leaders. Salespeople. Advertisers. If you stop and think, you will probably discover that at times your husband is manipulative. Adolescents definitely are. So why not you?

Manipulative or not, I have never hesitated to use Positive Reinforcement with my husband. Take the business of his making the coffee in the morning. For years I made it; but one day I bought a new coffeemaker that ground the beans as well as brewing the coffee. This caught Milt's eye. He loves gadgets and could not wait to try it out.

He brewed an experimental pot with coffee I had in the house. We agreed that it was a more efficient coffeemaker than our old one. The next night Milt came home with half a dozen bags of different kinds of coffee beans. He experimented for weeks, grinding different combinations of beans together until he hit on a blend that we both thought was superior. And he has made the coffee ever since.

He does not make it because he likes the gadgetry or because he thinks I don't make acceptable coffee; he makes it because he got a lot of Positive Reinforcement at the beginning, and eventually coffee-making became part of his morning routine without anything ever being said.

Every morning when he was experimenting with different blends, I sipped and pondered and gave him my reaction to that morning's brew. The morning he first brewed the mixture of beans that turned out to be our blend forever after, I told him he had attained perfection.

I still give him occasional doses of Positive Reinforcement. Recently I told him that if he should ever leave me for a younger woman, I planned to drop in on them every morning for coffee, because no one in the world makes coffee as good as his. He liked that bit of flattery a lot.

So the coffee-making is something that started very naturally. He made the initial move, but I nurtured his interest with lots of appreciation. Very sincere appreciation. It is wonderful to walk into the kitchen and be greeted by the aroma of freshly made coffee every morning.

Grocery shopping came about in much the same way. Years ago I was sitting at the kitchen table on a Saturday morning making out my shopping list. Milt wandered in and I said, "I'm going marketing. Want to come?"

It turned out he had nothing better to do. I went to work to make it fun for him. I introduced him to my favorite butcher, who was a vegetarian. The man at the fruit counter taught him how to pick out a ripe pineapple. When Milt spotted a bin of our favorite English muffins marked down to half price, he was triumphant and insisted we get six packages. We bought ice cream cones at the corner stand and staggered home juggling grocery bags and cones and chatting away about this, that and the other.

I really put myself out to be sure he enjoyed the shopping expedition. And he did. So did I. That is why I remember it so well. It was one of those wonderful days you never forget. We were in total harmony.

"We should do this more often," he said when I was putting our purchases away.

"It's a lot more fun doing it together than alone," I assured him.

I am not saying that from that day on Milt went grocery shopping with me every Saturday, but he went more often than not. And when he did, I did my best to make sure he enjoyed it.

Now that we spend most weekends on our farm, we always shop together. We stock up on staples at the mall and then we hit the farm stands. We buy eggs from a woman who lets her hens range free around the field, and we get our milk from a local dairy farmer. We are always discovering new places to get fresh produce.

These shared shopping expeditions do not give me more

time to myself. Nor do they save time. What they do give me—and Milt—is something far more precious. Time together doing something we enjoy. What used to be a solitary chore for me, something to be accomplished as fast as possible, has become a shared pleasure.

It was the country eggs that started Milt making breakfast on weekends. We are both city-born-and-bred. Having eggs that were practically fresh from the hen was something new. We had never dreamed that freshly laid eggs were so extraordinarily good.

I can't tell you how surprised I was the first morning on the farm when Milt said, "I'll do the eggs." When he slid his first fried egg out of the pan onto my plate, I told him it was a work of art. And when I tasted it, I told him it was the best fried egg I had ever eaten. The next thing I knew, Milt had taken over the whole breakfast routine—juice and coffee, toast and eggs, the works. He is never happier than when he is playing breakfast chef for a houseful of family and guests. And he never fails to get a big helping of Positive Reinforcement on those mornings.

Milt's most original culinary achievement, which far outshines his breakfasts in the estimation of his grandchildren, is gorilla sandwiches (grilled cheese to the rest of the world). I can't remember how gorilla sandwiches got started, but they are a menu staple when the grandchildren visit.

They involve a great deal of drama. Milt puts on a gorilla mask left from a long-ago Halloween and flaps around the kitchen roaring and imitating a gorilla as he slaps slices of cheese on the bread and puts them on the grill. The children are always enchanted. And that is Positive Reinforcement enough for anyone.

Would Milt have taken on his coffee-making and weekend breakfasts without my having used Positive Reinforcement? Absolutely not. Oh, he might have scrambled an occasional egg; but it is the praise and the appreciation that he received that established the behavior.

INTERMITTENT REINFORCEMENT

Positive Reinforcement and Operant Conditioning have their limits. If you hug your husband every single time he empties the dishwasher, your hugs will become devalued in a very short time. He will want more of a reward. A hug will no longer be enough to motivate him. So if you want him to keep on emptying the dishwasher, you have to escalate the scale of the reward. And how high can you go?

This is where Intermittent Reinforcement comes in. Scientists have learned that you can get more cooperation and more work out of someone whose best efforts go unrewarded as often as not.

Let me tell you about a second classic experiment with rats that illustrates the principle of Intermittent Reinforcement. A rat is put in that same empty cage with the same metal bar. This time, however, the mechanism is rigged to release a food pellet every fifth or sixth time the rat presses the bar instead of being released at every bar press.

The rat does not become discouraged by the uncertainty of the reward. Once he has associated hitting the metal bar with getting food, he will keep on hitting the bar time after time until he gets another food pellet. Each time he gets food, this reinforces his hit-the-bar behavior enough to keep him bumping that bar again and again even though he is not rewarded each time.

How does one apply Intermittent Reinforcement to that dishwasher-emptying husband? The first time he empties the dishwasher, give him that hug. Show him your approval and appreciation. The second time he empties it, give him another hug. But the third time—zip! Nothing. The fourth time—nothing again. But the fifth calls for a hug. You can take it from there. Every fourth or fifth time would probably be the appropriate interval, just enough to keep him motivated until the behavior becomes habit. Then your reinforcement can be even more intermittent.

Intermittent Reinforcement can be used in many circumstances. Suppose you have a valued employee—a secretary, a researcher, a housekeeper, a baby-sitter. You want that person to keep working for you. You want to show you appreciate that person's dependability and ingenuity. An occasional compliment will be more effective than a steady stream of flattery. Someone told me once that one of the secretaries at NBC complained that her head hurt from so much patting by her appreciative boss.

A pay increase is always welcome, but too many or too generous increases may have the opposite effect of what you intend. A study by Professor John Mirowsky of the University of Illinois revealed that frequent increases in pay, no matter how generous, tend to bolster an employee's belief that he or she deserves even more. The result can be resentment rather than satisfaction. Your cherished housekeeper or secretary or baby-sitter may go looking for another position where she (or he) will be more highly appreciated.

One woman who attended an executive seminar in which I was outlining the theory of Operant Conditioning asked, "Why should the wife have to be the one who has to provide Positive and Intermittent Reinforcement?"

"Who else?" I asked in reply. "The wife is the one who wants the change."

Some men seem genetically resistant to change. No kind of Operant Conditioning will get them to do the dishes or wax the floor. If you don't have household help, you are stuck with the housework. It is not fair. As Nancy Evans says, "There is no getting around the fact that working women need wives."

Way back in the first issue of *Ms.* magazine, Judy Syfers, who described herself as belonging to "that classification of people known as wives," wrote, "One evening it suddenly occurred to me that I, too, would like to have a wife.

"I want a wife who will keep my house clean . . . pick up after me . . . keep my clothes clean, ironed, mended . . . a wife who is a good cook . . . who will care for me when I'm sick . . . who will not bother me with rambling complaints about a wife's duties . . . who is sensitive to my sexual needs . . ."

I want a wife too, but wives for women is an idea whose time has not yet come. When all is said and done, most working wives end up doing more than their husbands. Let me just point out the silver lining to this cloud, but I advise you to keep it to yourself. It is one of those bits of knowledge that are best confined to the female sex.

Two University of California sociologists, William and Denise Bielby, who analyzed data from a nationwide survey of working men and women, found that the women worked harder and spent more time on their jobs than the men, despite the fact that the women also worked harder and spent more time on household tasks than the men. "For women to work harder than men, despite their greater household responsibilities," the Bielbys concluded, they must have an energy reserve that "is either not available to the typical male or that men choose not to draw upon."

The first—that women have a greater energy reserve—is the more likely answer according to physiological research. Women are stronger than men in significant ways. Men have a higher proportion of muscle to fat than women do, which gives them more physical strength, but women's fat reserves give them more long-term energy. And in today's world, we need energy more than sheer brute force.

To understand this business of energy, take runners. When a runner complains that he "hit the wall," he is talking about the excruciating pain and weakness that suddenly hits him when he has used up all his glycogen. Glycogen is the form in which carbohydrates are stored in muscles. A runner who puts out roughly 80 percent of his or her top effort will use up the glycogen in his or her muscles in about two hours, possibly sooner. At this point, he or she "hits the wall." A man can keep on running for a little longer, but he slows down dramatically. A woman's body switches over to her fat reserves for fuel. Gram for gram, fat provides more than twice as much energy as glycogen. A woman's sex hormones help her muscles use her fat more easily than men's muscles can (and remember, they have less fat anyway), with the result that women can keep on going long after a man drops by the wayside.

Women retain this energy edge throughout their lives. Their capacity for exercise, for instance, exceeds that of men. Treadmill tests have shown that a man's capacity drops about 10 percent for every ten years of age. A woman's drops only 2 percent.

So if you are doing more than your share, you should know that you are capable of putting out more energy both at work and at home than your spouse. I do not offer this as consolation; but it is worth remembering that in many ways that count, you are stronger than that man you married. As I said earlier, it may be wise to keep this to yourself.

ELEVEN

SUCCESSFUL WOMEN set their priorities and refuse to get side-tracked by time-wasting trivia. As I talked with them, I found that most followed three cardinal rules both at home and at work. Delegate. Organize. Concentrate. No matter what your family, financial or career situation, these rules can help you squeeze more time out of the day for yourself.

DELEGATE

Supersuccessful Helen Gurley Brown says every working woman must remember four words. "And put those words in capitals," she instructed. "DON'T GO THERE YOUR-SELF!!!"

"This means that you do not go to the store," she says. "You do not go to the dry cleaner. You do not go anywhere to pick something up or drop something off. Someone else does.

"I have a wonderful assistant in the office. She is going to Charles Jourdan this afternoon to buy me a pair of shoes. I have one pair in the right size. She is going to pick up a second pair in another color. Until recently I would have done this myself, but day after day, week after week, year after year, I have figured out more things that other people can do for me.

"I used to plan our menus and give them to the house-keeper until one day she said, 'Why don't you let me do this? I know how to plan a meal. Anything I can do for you, I don't want you to touch.' And I thought, *You're damn right!* No more of this business of I'll just dab a little polish on these shoes, or straighten up the bed before I leave, or sew on this snap. No! No! NAUGHTY! NAUGHTY!!! I have learned to let my housekeeper do it. And I have no guilt.

"I hardly ever go shopping. Most of my clothes come from Calvin Klein and Adolfo. I go to their shows. That takes an hour once or twice a year, when I see everything that they have. Then I call and order what I want. I also order things that I see in the ads from Saks Fifth Avenue by telephone. I can't spare the time to go there, although it's less than a mile from my office, so I order by telephone. That is, my assistant orders by telephone.

"Now, everyone does not have a housekeeper or a wonderful assistant," Helen went on, "but there are things every woman can do. For instance, maybe you can hire a high school girl who wants to make some money on Saturdays. Save up fifteen things for her to do. Those are fifteen things you won't have to do."

Household help, whether it is full-time or part-time or just three or four hours a week, can make all the difference. But what if even a high school girl on Saturday mornings is out of the question? There are many solutions to this problem.

Dr. Marilyn Manning of Los Altos, California, a psychologist who holds seminars on conflict and stress management for universities and corporations, found ways.

"We live in a town with a community college," she said. "I

always had a college student living with us when the children were little. They baby-sat and cooked and cleaned in return for their room and board. We both gained by this very inexpensive arrangement. I don't understand why more women don't try this.

"These days my kids do all the housecleaning. We take turns with the cooking. I do the laundry and my husband does the shopping. I trained my husband and children in operating an equal household. I don't think it just happens. There was a lot of resistance; but it was worth the effort."

Marilyn Moore, an executive at Frito-Lay in Dallas, says, "Most of the housecleaning is done by the three children. We have a schedule, a rotating schedule that changes once a week," she said.

"The chores are divided into three different levels. The first-level person has the easy chores, the third-level person the hard ones. The second has the in-between ones. The first-level person gets to choose the television program, gets to sit in the front seat, choose the dessert, that kind of thing. And the third-level person always knows that next week will be easier.

"They don't always do things exactly the way I would, but they do real well. And I accept that. That's part of the deal. I don't have time to go after them and revacuum the living room. It's not that important to me to have every speck of dust up."

Angela Shute (a pseudonym for a woman who requested anonymity) has her own insurance agency in the Los Angeles area. "My husband and I and our twelve-year-old daughter clean house Sunday nights," she reported. "We could afford to hire someone, but I just don't like the idea of another woman cleaning my house. So what we do is the three of us work all out for three hours—from five to eight—every Sunday night. That's nine hours of work. We do everything.

Change the beds, scrub the bathrooms, do the laundry, the ironing, make the kitchen sparkle. Everything.

"And every week, we each do something extra. My daughter will dust a couple of bookshelves. I might clean out the fridge or do some mending or repot some of the plants on the patio or wash a room's worth of curtains. My husband usually washes windows. On the dot of eight, the timer goes off and we're through. That's it for the week.

"Afterwards we take showers, order in Chinese food or a pizza and watch a movie on the VCR while we eat. When the movie is over, we're off to bed. We have a good time Sunday nights. Cleaning house is one of those things where you can see the results. And as my daughter says, 'We three make a great team.' "

These are all relatively painless ways to get work done, even if you don't have outside help. Any woman who lives in a college town might do well to investigate the possibility of having a live-in student to help out. I think both the rotating chore schedule and the work-against-the-clock plan are truly inspired.

Children are obviously a great resource once they are old enough to help, but these schemes work as well for husband and wife. The important consideration in all of these solutions is that whether you rely on a housekeeper or a live-in student or your spouse or your children, you have delegated at least half of the domestic responsibilities.

ORGANIZE

Successful women are excellent organizers. Most of them maintain that the key to good organization is a list—or lists.

"I keep lists," says Gillian Sorensen. "I have an office list, a home list, a to-do list for the week, a long-range list, an A list and a B list. I cross things off and I move them up. I'm always juggling, keeping things moving forward. I review the lists every week and that's how things get done.

"My daughter, Juliet, teases me. She will ask me about something and I will say, 'It's on my list.' It may not get done immediately, but the important things do. Having laundry done and food in the house is crucial. Reorganizing my closets, that can wait. It's not crucial."

The minute you have a list, you are in control. You see your priorities right there in front of you. You arrange and rearrange them to suit the circumstances. And each time you cross something off your list, you get a feeling of achievement. It is a kind of mini-success.

My own life is a constant process of triage, of making emergency decisions on what is most important, must be done first, absolutely cannot wait. Without my lists, I would be lost.

Every night before I go to bed, I write down the three things that *must* be done the next day. And then the ten or twelve or twenty things that *should* be done the next day. My third list contains things that will have to be done soon. It is like an Early Warning Alarm.

I try to handle the big three on my list the first thing in the morning. If I manage to cross off all three, it is a triumph. I squeeze the items on my secondary list in between appointments. I manage to get in a lot of telephoning at airports while I'm between planes. I think of a plane as a second office. I get a lot of reading and writing done on planes. That is how most of this book was written; but I am as likely to be making out a grocery list as outlining an article or working on a speech. It all depends upon the priority of the moment.

At the end of the day I go over the lists. I never get everything done, but I always get some things done, and eventually everything does get done—or I end up by dropping it from my list. Like exercising for half an hour every day. I've given that up as hopeless.

Sybil Ferguson, the founder of Diet Center, Inc., is another woman who copes with a hectic life by means of lists. She travels almost constantly, visiting Diet Centers across the country and promoting her books, and she manages her household in Rexburg, Idaho, with the help of several high school girls. She has detailed lists for each of them outlining their duties. Why several girls? Well, Sybil has a very large house. She and her husband bought it before she started Diet Center, and in order to pay for it, she took in college boys as boarders. "I had seventeen college boys and my own five children, so you can see that this is a house that could not be run with someone coming in for a few hours a week.

"I make lists for myself too," she says. "It's a very effective way of getting things done. And I recommend that all my Diet Center counselors make lists. Lists make life simpler."

Shopping is another great time consumer. Like Helen Gurley Brown, I rarely go shopping. I buy most of my clothes from catalogues. There are many excellent mail-order catalogues now, and they are a great time-saver. Not just for clothes, but for kitchen utensils, bedding, furniture, all kinds of things.

I spend very little time or thought on my clothes. A few years ago I did a series of television shows for Trevira, and they had a wonderful stylist, China Machado, put my wardrobe together. She made me lists of what to wear with what. And I find them very useful. You don't have to stop and think. I am still wearing a lot of the clothes she chose for me, and when I buy new clothes, I work out my own lists, so I always know exactly what I am going to wear with what.

Lynn Gilbert, partner in Tweed and Gilbert, an international executive-search firm, is a woman who likes to shop, but does not like to waste time shopping. She has worked out a solution. "The only time I spend any time going shopping," she says, "is when I'm traveling on business. If I'm in Dallas and I have an appointment at nine and the next one isn't until three, there is nothing I can do in between. I can't talk with my daughter. I can't write a business proposal. So I go shopping. It's the only time I can shop without guilt."

Possibly the most important list a working woman can make for herself is a Network List. We all know about networking for career advancement, for information and for contacts. Women also need domestic networks, support systems to help them deal with their lives.

We all need people we can call on in an emergency. You fall and break your leg and have to be taken to the hospital. Your husband is out of town on a business trip. Whom can you call to pick up your car in the downtown garage and drive it home for you? Whom can you call to come in and get supper for the kids that night? You need people you can muster when the dishwasher is leaking, the cellar is flooded, the lawn mower has given up the ghost, the dog is having convulsions, your child is sent home from school sick. You need a list of electricians, plumbers, repairmen, mechanics, veterinarians, baby-sitters, as well as of friends and neighbors and family members you can call on in emergencies. And you need that list at your fingertips.

My daughter, Lisa, has what she calls her Security Network. She has a child-care person and a housecleaning person, a retired man who will come in and wait for the plumber or the furnace repairman. She has high school girls who will take things that need to be repaired and pick them up afterwards, return things that don't work or don't fit and run all sorts of errands for her.

And she has the grandparent network. Milt and I are available for short-term panics, since we are closer. We fly out and baby-sit and cook whenever we are needed. When Lisa was pregnant with her third child, there was a time when she needed to just put her legs up for a few days and take it easy, and Milt and I took over the house and the children and the coddling Lisa needed for those few days. The other grandparents are available for long-term crises. When the whole house had to be rewired, they came and stayed throughout the invasion of the electricians.

With her Security Network, Lisa knows that if the ground opens up, there is always someone she can turn to.

I have city and country Network Lists. Since we are at our farm only on weekends and during our vacation, I have to have people I can really depend on to check that the furnace is working in the depths of winter, to let the television repairman in, to take delivery of packages. Without my neighborhood network, I would be in trouble. On the summer day a murderous thunderstorm knocked out the power, a good neighbor transferred the contents of my freezer to her generator-powered freezer.

My banker is an important part of my network. I have a woman banker I have known ever since she was a beginning teller. Whenever she has been promoted and moved to another branch I have transferred my account to wherever she is. She makes sure that I never bounce a check. If I need money moved from my account to Milt's or from his to mine (and we move money back and forth all the time) she takes care of it. I hardly ever have to set foot inside the bank.

A few years ago, just before my dad died, our whole family went to Nassau, in the Caribbean. It was a special time, because we knew Dad would not be with us much longer, and we spent far more money than we'd expected on doing everything that we knew he liked. When we ran out of money, I telephoned my banker in New York. She recognized my voice, and when I mentioned a couple of details that only she and I knew, she was able to send money. I can't begin to count the hours that this wonderful woman has saved me over the years.

Working wives and mothers have triggered a whole new industry, a personal-service industry composed of people who—for a fee—will do those chores you don't have time or energy for. One agency in New York will wait in line for you at the Passport Office or the Motor Vehicle Bureau. Another agency will do everything from planning your meals to reorganizing your files to paying your bills. There are household-management agencies that will pick up and deliver laundry and dry cleaning, baby-sit, mail packages, deliver meals, shop for groceries, weed the garden, wait in your home for repairmen and deliveries, take your car to be serviced.

If you live in or near a big city, you will find dozens of these agencies listed in the Yellow Pages. They are worth checking out for your Network List. One day one of them might be just the port you need in a storm. A Network List is a time and energy saver. A Network List is emergency insurance. If you don't have one, start building your personal network right now so you will have the names and numbers you need when you need them.

CONCENTRATION

What interested me as I spoke with successful women was how often older women would refer back to the time they spent at home running the house and raising children as wonderful preparation for their professional lives. They all reported that they had developed the ability to concentrate fiercely on whatever they were doing and to shift the focus of their concentration very rapidly when necessary to another subject or problem and concentrate on that just as intensely.

When Jeane Kirkpatrick talked about her years as Ambassador to the United Nations, she said, "It was a fourteen-hour day, a seven-day week, a fifty-two-week year. I gave up everything except occasions like Christmas with my family.

"I had to make the most efficient use of my time. I think that some capacities that I developed in the course of being an active mother of active boys and also pursuing a professional life outside the home helped me in those United Nations years.

"There are many skills one develops and hones as the mother of a family and manager of a household that are useful professionally—and almost always ignored. You do a number of quite different activities simultaneously. I learned when I was home with the boys to make very efficient use of my time, to transfer my focus of attention very rapidly and to think very intensively. I learned to make intensive use of the time available to me."

Felice Schwartz feels the same way about her years at home. "I stayed home for eight years after my second child was born. I had three children in those years, I was working at home to set up Catalyst. One of the tremendous things it did for me—and I am sure it did for other women—is that while I was doing all of those mechanical things around the house, I learned how to think and plan, to concentrate.

"When I sit down to write, I'm ready. It just flows out. I have it all thought through, because that is what I had to do while I was loading the dishwasher and the clothes washer and mowing the lawn and taking care of the kids. When my husband sits down to write, he doesn't start to think until he picks up the pencil."

A survey of 164 men and 38 women in management positions carried out by psychologist Lynn Offerman of George Washington University found that women use more time-management techniques than men. Women are better than men are at organizing jobs by priority and scheduling important jobs for times of peak energy.

Dr. Phyllis Harrison-Ross learned how to use time-management techniques early on. "I have dyslexia," she said, "and when I was in medical school, I found that I was going to have to concentrate if I was going to get through the enormous amount of material first-year medical students have to learn.

"Because of the dyslexia, my eyes were so tired at the end of the day that I found it hard to absorb information when I studied at night. I learned to work around my disability. If I had something that demanded intense concentration, I attacked it between five and seven in the morning. This is a practice I still follow.

"Later on, as director of the Community Mental Health Center at Metropolitan Hospital, where I had a lot of administrative duties, I found that I was constantly subject to interruptions. These disrupted my train of thought, slowed up my work and generally frustrated me until I realized that interruptions were part of my job.

"Once I accepted that, I was able to maintain my concentration. I could switch off from whatever I was doing and concentrate on whatever the problem was that caused the interruption and then switch back to what I was doing with the same intense concentration. I no longer let my resentment of interruptions interfere with my concentration."

I have always found it easy to concentrate. "When Joyce is reading," my mother used to say, "you could light a bomb under her chair and she wouldn't know." Once as a child I was thinking so intensely about something that I walked right past my grandmother on the street without seeing her.

For those people who were not born with a bump of concentration, there are two physical aids to concentration that you can use to advantage: standing up and lying down.

If you have something that you must learn or a problem that you must solve right here and now, you will concentrate better if you work on it standing up. I have never had a desk in my study. I stand at a table, with whatever material I need to refer to on the table. And I always stand when I have an important telephone call.

If you have a long-term problem that demands concentrated thought and careful weighing of alternative solutions, you will concentrate better lying down. I usually retreat to a warm bath when I have this kind of problem. My body is completely relaxed and my mind free to consider all aspects of a situation, review the implications of different approaches and come up with a solution that feels right.

The time of optimum concentration varies from individual to individual. Chronobiologists have found that everyone has approximately four hours of peak mental efficiency a day.

A friend of mine who writes novels told me, "I used to feel terribly guilty. I would wander around the house all morning, knowing I should sit down at the typewriter and get to work. But when I sat down, I just didn't produce. I would accuse myself of being lazy, worry that I would never be able to write another word and feel generally miserable.

"Finally, around one or two in the afternoon, I would whip

myself into going into my study and getting to work. And I would really work—three or four, sometimes five hours. The next day I would go through the whole routine again.

"When you told me about everyone having those four peak hours of mental activity, all my guilt vanished. My peak hours were obviously afternoon hours. I no longer feel I have to put in an eight-hour day at the typewriter. I settle down at one in the afternoon and tell myself that my four peak hours are ahead of me. It's time to get to work. Once I get started, momentum sometimes keeps me going for five or six hours."

How can you pinpoint your own four peak hours? If you stop and think about the pattern of your days, you probably can spot the span of hours when you get most done and your mind is sharpest. If you are not sure, chart your temperature for a couple of weeks. A person's peak hours usually start about an hour before her temperature reaches its highest point of the day. Most people concentrate best in the morning, but there are those whose optimum time is in the afternoon or even at night.

There are several kinds of concentration. There is what I call "attentive" concentration. This is the kind of concentration Ambassador Kirkpatrick spoke of—when your mind is sharply focused on one subject and then can switch its focus rapidly to be equally intensely focused on another subject.

A second kind of concentration is known as "flow." Dr. Mihaly Csikszentmihaly, a psychologist at the University of Chicago, has been studying flow for more than a decade. He describes it as a kind of "mental overdrive. There is a mental recruitment where everything aligns in an effortless concentration.

"People seem to concentrate best," he has found, "when the demands on them are a bit greater than usual and they are able to give more than usual. If there is too little demand on them, people are bored. If there is too much for them to handle, they get anxious. Flow occurs in that delicate zone between boredom and anxiety."

It is a state of total involvement. My favorite example of

flow is the surgeon who was so deeply involved in the surgery he was performing that he was completely unaware that part of the operating-room ceiling collapsed halfway through the operation. Only after the incision was closed did he straighten up, stretch and look around. "What's all that plaster on the floor?" he asked.

A person usually enters a state of flow when working on something difficult that demands total attention over a period of hours. It is rare that anyone attains a flow state in less than half an hour. Once it is attained it can last for several hours.

And then there is "strained" concentration, which occurs when you force yourself to concentrate on something that interests you very little or not at all. Researchers at the National Institute of Mental Health have discovered that the brain functions differently in flow and strained concentration. In flow, cortical arousal is decreased. In strained concentration, it is increased—almost as if, as Daniel Goleman of *The New York Times* put it, "the brain is in the wrong gear for the work demanded."

So there you are. Delegate. Organize. Concentrate. If you follow these three rules, you can do anything. Or almost anything. And if you think I am placing too much emphasis on making the most of your time, let me share a discouraging bit of information: Everything takes longer than you think it will. According to an algebraic analysis worked out by Philip Musgrove which appeared in *American Economic Review*, things take 2.71828 times longer than you think they will; so you see, there is no time to waste.

TWELVE

A FRIEND of mine once spent an evening with actress Louise Fletcher, who won an Oscar for her role in *One Flew over the Cuckoo's Nest,* in Louise's parents' home in Birmingham, Alabama. Her mother and father had gone to bed. The two women had been talking far through the night and into the morning. Finally they were silent. There was not a sound in the house but the tock-tock-tock of the old grandfather clock. "I hate that sound," Louise said. "It is the saddest sound in the world. A bit of your life gone with every tick." An actress, mother, wife and devoted daughter to her deaf parents, Louise saw time as her enemy. There was never enough. And it went by so fast, so irrevocably.

For many working wives, time is the enemy of sex. There is never enough time for sex.

"Sex?" says executive Karol Emmerich. "Sure there are time pressures. Anybody who works has time pressures. You are tired all the time. Does my husband complain? Who's got time to complain?"

And editor Jacqueline Leo says, "I'm tired and it affects our sexual life. He complains sometimes that we don't have enough time for sex, but he is understanding. He is tired too. I suppose he might even be tempted to look around at times, but if he did, I'd kill him. We have made choices and must stick to them and support each other."

It is not only successful women leading high-pressured lives who find that sex is a problem. Columnist Ann Landers reports that there has been a definite change in emphasis in her mail in recent years. The emphasis has switched to the problems of dual-career couples, especially their sexual problems.

"Sex has become a definite problem," she says, "when both the man and the woman are working. The woman is tired. She is holding down two jobs—contributing to the family income and taking care of the house and children. She's exhausted at the end of the day. This does not bode well for lovemaking."

The women I and my researchers interviewed fell into three categories when it came to sex. Sex was a major problem, a minor problem or no problem at all in their marriages.

Major Problem Their husbands complained that they did not have sex often enough. This was a major issue in the marriage.

Minor Problem The women reported that their careers interfered with their sex lives. Lack of time and fatigue were the problems. Husbands and wives put their heads together to find solutions to what they considered a joint problem. It was not a major issue in the marriage. Most women were in this category.

No Problem at All These women reported that they had wonderful sex lives and a good marital relationship. They could not ask for anything better.

MAJOR PROBLEM

The first situation was demonstrably destructive to the marriages in this sample. The husbands complained that their wife's job meant more to her than they did. The complaints were along these lines: Night after night after night, your husband wanted to make love, but

A. You just walked in the door with a briefcase full of work. The latest Wall Street scandal shook the powers-that-be in your office and you have to produce a report on who traded what and when for tomorrow morning's meeting. You have no time for lovemaking. You will be lucky if you even see your bed tonight.

B. That creep down the hall pulled a fast one at the marketing meeting this afternoon. He suggested that he take over one of your Dayton accounts because he heard there were complaints that you had not visited them lately. It's true. For the last month you have been completely absorbed in landing the JJJ account. And you got it. You should fly to Dayton tomorrow to mend your fences. This means spending tonight reviewing the unhappy account and coming up with something wonderful to make up for your temporary lapse of attention.

C. You are just plain exhausted.

He points out that there are always crises in your life. And nights when you don't drag work home, you are always too tired to do more than go to bed and stare at a sitcom on the tube.

He is right. But what are you to do? You are ambitious. You have a demanding and exciting job. You have been knocking yourself out to get ahead or stay ahead. Why can't he understand?

He does understand. He understands that you can be too tired. He understands that there are times when you have to bring work home. This does not mean that he likes it. And it does not mean that he is not going to complain, although if he only knew, his complaining may make things worse.

One thing that even the most sensitive man does not seem to comprehend is that he can complain that he is not getting enough sex until he is blue in the face, but it won't get him what he wants. All he is doing is providing Negative Reinforcement. A woman may say, "Oh, all right," and have sex to pacify him, but in time this sex-as-duty becomes a sexual turn-off and can totally inhibit a woman's desire.

The fact is that he feels somewhat rejected, feels that he is being relegated to second place. And this is hard. Men really want to be dominant. He wants to make it clear that he is cock of the walk even though you are a big success and earn top dollar. Having sex when he wants it is one of the important ways in which he convinces himself of his dominance. Remember that study I described in Chapter Four showing that men feel inadequate when their wives work? When a man cannot have sex on demand with his working wife the way he is sure his father did with his nonworking wife, he feels even more inadequate.

Most of the time his feelings are right on target. As far as his wife's priorities go, he is definitely in second place.

Here are three cases where not-enough-sex was a major issue in a successful woman's marriage. The names, careers, and geographical locations of the women have been heavily disguised, but their words are verbatim.

"The best way I can put it is that sex is the last thing on my list of things to do," said Chloe Sharpe, a top literary agent who has been married to a successful retailer for three years.

"With all the commitments I have in the course of a day, when I get home at night I just want to relax. Lie down for a while. I bring a lot of manuscripts home that I have to read before I go back to the office in the morning. I want quiet time alone, and that causes a problem. I am not ready to connect with my husband on any level when I get home.

"What happens is we have dinner and we talk and after that I am just not inclined to have sex. It is very hard. He complains, and we talk about it a lot. But we don't seem to have solved anything."

Kelly Martin is a partner in a machine-tool firm in Phoenix, Arizona, and her husband is an accountant. "He complains that we don't have sex often enough," Kelly said. "By the time I hit the sack, I'm not ready for play. I'm ready for sleep. I'm tired, and he doesn't understand why.

"I explain to him that we move at a different pace and this is why I'm tired and he isn't. I move very fast all day from the minute I wake up. I hardly ever sit down. He walks slower than I walk. He talks slower than I talk. He does everything slower than I do."

Kelly was interested when I told her about a study of 200 adults and 100 children in Lincoln, Nebraska, which found that women walk faster than men. Professor Michael Hill, a sociologist and geographer, ascertained that on the average, women walk at the rate of 256 feet a minute and men at a rate of 245 feet a minute.

"If we have gone several days without sex," Kelly continued, "even if I don't feel like it, I will. I do it because I can tell how he is feeling. He is feeling rejected. There are times, though, when the complaints build up and I don't do anything about it. Then he gets worse and worse and worse. The way he relates to the whole family changes. He is not pleasant to be around."

Jill Edmunds, who does public relations for film personalities, was married to a top executive of a Fortune 500 company for twelve years. A recent divorcee, Jill said, "In our situation, my career started to take priority over our marriage, and that is what eventually eroded what had been a very strong bond.

"The sexual complaint was very deep. In the beginning I denied it. I said, 'That's ridiculous. You know that I am always here for you.' I did not pay attention to what was really true, which was that I was putting my work ahead of my husband.

How I handled the problem was to avoid it for far too long. When I finally faced it, I realized how unfair I had been to a man who needed priority."

In these three cases, the women chose to put their careers first, their marriages second. The trade-off for Jill and Kelly has been divorce. Kelly instituted divorce proceedings several months after this interview. To these women and significant numbers of other women, marriage is a humdrum affair compared with their work, which they find challenging and rewarding. More rewarding than marriage.

Actually, marriage seems to be less appealing to many women these days. A recent survey designed to find out what women considered most enjoyable about being female showed that only 6 percent of the women who participated assigned first place to being a wife. A career, a paycheck, motherhood and "general rights and freedoms" were rated as more enjoyable than marriage and wifehood.

This fits in with what many women have told me: that they get more satisfaction—more "warm fuzzies," as one woman put it—from their work than from their marriages. But why not? Men always have. Work can be a very seductive mistress.

In mid-1968, *The Wall Street Journal* reported on a group of successful young men. For all of them, as psychiatrist Samuel Klagsbrun of Katonah, New York, said, business was God. It took precedence over their wives, children, hobbies and free time.

For example, one man who had a wife and three children earned more than a million dollars a year. He worked eighty-hour weeks and had been known to go on three-day "work binges" when he never set foot outside the office. Another successful Wall Streeter reported that he had not taken a day off in the last ten months. It was not only money that drove these men, but the challenge of competition, the desire to prove themselves.

"Most men do put their work first," says Joni Evans, former president of Simon and Schuster's Trade Division, now with Random House. "That doesn't mean that they don't love their wives. Women should be able to say, 'I put my work first, but that doesn't mean I don't love you.' "

Men have always derived their identities from their work. "I am a salesman . . . an accountant . . . a pilot . . . a mechanic . . . a broker." Women have derived their identity from their husbands and families. "She's Calvin's wife . . . Karen's mother . . . Ramon's wife . . . Jeff's mom." Today's successful women are carving out new identities for themselves. Some are choosing to put their careers first, and they are having to make trade-offs, often cruel trade-offs.

When Liz Roman Gallese researched what had happened to the women of the class of 1975 at Harvard Business School, whom she described as the first women to have a chance to make it to the top in the corporate world, she got in touch with each of the 88 women who had been enrolled in the class. She found that it was the rare woman who was tops in her career field who had a satisfactory marriage with a man she respected. In her book, *Women Like Us*, Gallese concluded that there are "certain realities about forming a career in today's business world . . . One must put that career first, before husbands, even before children, however harsh that may sound."

Men do not need to choose between career and family, because the majority of highly successful men usually have a wife to take care of the personal sphere of their lives. But the woman who wants both a career and marriage must be prepared to chart her own way in what is still largely unexplored territory. She is a twentieth-century pioneer.

MINOR PROBLEM

For the women in the second group, those who reported that their work interfered with their sex lives, the problem is time more than priorities. Sex is not a major issue in their marriages. Many see it as a temporary problem. When the children are older, when they can afford more help around the house, when job demands taper off, when this or that happens, then there will be time for sex. In the meantime, they live their lives and make time for each other as best they can. Their solutions to finding time for sex are ingenious and practical. Their attitudes are equally practical. As workaholic Helen Gurley Brown said, "It is very hard to make time for sex, but you just have to make up your mind not to give it up. You have to work it out somehow."

The way most couples work it out is by making dates to be together, scheduling time for sex and trying to be as flexible as possible. Planning is the key.

Lana Jane Lewis-Brent, president and chief executive officer of the Sunshine Jr. Stores chain, who lives in Panama City, Florida, says, "My busy life does not particularly affect our sex life, except that it is probably more planned than some other people's might be, just like a lot of things with our hectic schedules."

There are people who scoff at the idea of scheduling time for sex. "Sex should be spontaneous," they say. "You can't schedule sex like a dentist's appointment or taking the car to be serviced."

They are wrong. You can. Sex researchers Masters and Johnson strongly recommend making time to be together regularly. They warn that sexual desire may decline if a couple do not have unencumbered pockets of private time together.

Just look back to the early days of your relationship when you knew that a date would probably end—and possibly begin—in lovemaking. Did that make it any less exciting? The truth is that anticipation adds to the excitement. A study was done some years ago on just when—what days of the week—people made love. It turned out, rather surprisingly, that the most popular night for sex was Tuesday—except for the medical profession. Most doctors, the study revealed, make love on Saturday nights, the one night in the week when they are least likely to be interrupted. I can confirm that knowing what was on the agenda for Saturdays never took any of the pleasure away.

"We don't have enough time for sex," says Linda Tarry, president of her own computer consulting company, Database Network. "We both feel that way. What we do is we both sit down and say, 'What are we going to schedule for next week?' If sex is going to be a priority, we put it in the book for, say, Wednesday and Saturday nights.

"We try to get away every now and then. We make sure that the children are scheduled for a certain number of weekends with Grandma during the year. And we always take at least one major vacation without the children, usually in the winter."

"We plan time together," says Linda Grant, who lives in a New York suburb. "We go into New York City on weekends. Take a hotel room. I have a premed student who comes and baby-sits Joshua for me when we do this."

"It is really hard to have time together when the children are so little," says Karen Nussbaum. "Sex is one of the things we wish there were more time for.

"What works for us is to occasionally take a day off from work. I take the children to day care as usual, but we stay home. This way we have time to spend with each other when we are feeling energetic and not all washed out the way we are at night. This is something we enjoy a lot. Sometimes we go out to lunch. Other times we may do things like putting up the screens or any of the jobs we never have time for when the children are around. Or sometimes we just plain do nothing. It is a nice way to spend a day. I think it ends up making a difference."

Heloise says, "David does complain, usually when I've been traveling a lot and then come home absolutely exhausted, that we don't have sex often enough. I should not really say he complains. It is more a question of, 'What are we going to do about this?' Some people say they have sex on an average of five or seven times a week. Those are people who live together and whose jobs don't take them away from home. People like me—well, when you think that I'm away for three days and then I'm home for two and then I'm gone for five and home for six, how do you figure out the frequency then? Except that it's never enough.

"I wish we had more time just for us. My office is in our home and David shares part of it, but we're not necessarily together. He's on the phone and I'm on the phone and he's running out and that kind of thing. What we need is more time away from home together.

"One thing we do is I travel extensively and if I have a speaking engagement on a Thursday or Friday, David will meet me wherever it is and then we will spend the weekend together. Like next week, we are going to go to Mexico. That is our real special time to be together, stashed away in a hotel room with room service.

"I think it's vital to spend time away from home. Even if you send the kids to Grandma, the dogs are there and the phone rings and you suddenly notice all the plants need watering. One idea, if you can't afford to go to a hotel or a motel, is to swap houses with someone. You don't have to spend a lot of money if you do this, and it gets you right away from all your own responsibilities. Part of what makes some love affairs so exciting is that they are in a borrowed apartment. Like married couples who want to make love with someone else—they borrow someone's apartment to use during the lunch hour or after work. There was a movie about that."

Some of the busiest women work hardest at nurturing their marriages and making time for sex. Chris Boe Voran made time together with her husband one of her priorities. As a corporate lawyer, she often worked twelve- and fourteen-hour days, while her husband kept normal hours and left his office at seven every night.

"I disliked immensely not having dinner with him. I also disliked coming home from work after he was already in bed.

This meant I really didn't get a chance to see him or talk to him that day.

"To solve the problem, what I did was pack my briefcase and go home at seven too. I would cook dinner. We would eat together. I would clean up and we would have time together. When he went to sleep, I would go into my little home study and work until three or four or five in the morning. I was burning the candle at both ends, but it was important to have time with my husband."

Pat Collins, who now heads her own production company, said, "When I was at WCBS, Joe's and my hours were completely different. We would only see each other at obligatory social events, even though we lived under the same roof. And that's no good. Just try to have a conversation with your husband in a room with three hundred other people all drinking Chablis!

"On weekends I felt so guilty for not having been around for the children that I tended to pour all my attention onto the kids, and Joe was really left at the end of the line. He would complain.

"We try to play catch-up on our sex life. We'll say, 'We absolutely have to have a weekend together.' And we manage it. Somehow.

"I remember one of those weekends. We went to what we thought was going to be a charming old New England inn. When we got there, we could not believe it. The room had a naked light bulb hanging from the center of the ceiling. The screens for the windows were stacked in the bathroom. The bedspread looked and felt like oilcloth. And we discovered we had to share the bathroom with another couple.

"Here was our big weekend. And here we were in this dump! It was so awful we had to laugh. We sat on the floor and laughed. And then we got back in the car, went someplace for dinner and pulled into our driveway at home at one in the morning. Much to the shock of everyone.

"We live outside the city," Pat says, "so when we drive home together, that is a chance for time alone. And we have a house on Cape Cod where we go for vacations. When we are there we always try to do something—a bike ride or a trip to the hardware store—where we can be alone together without the children. It is very small-scale time, but unless you do that, you don't have anything.

"We had dinner alone not long ago, and Joe took out his appointment book and flipped through the weeks and months. Finally he said, 'Do you know it was February eighth the last time we had dinner alone?' And this was September!"

Even vacation planning can be difficult for dual-career couples. Not that they can't agree on where to go or what to do: it is time that messes them up. According to one survey, 28 percent of dual-career couples take shorter vacations than they did when they were single, mostly because it is so hard for husband and wife to get vacations in the same time slot.

Susan Steiner (not her real name) is a certified public accountant. Her vacation cannot conflict with the tax season. She also must coordinate with the children's school vacations. And with her husband's vacations. Her husband is a banker, and bank policy dictates that executives with one-month vacations must take the time in separate two-week chunks.

"I run it through the computer," Susan said. "The tax season. The children. Irving's two weeks. Our vacation windows are always very narrow."

The women in this category want to give their husbands and marriages priority, but there are times when career demands and household responsibilities dictate otherwise. The willingness of these couples to compromise and their obvious desire for each other's happiness seem to keep these marriages loving and stable even when sex is a sometime thing.

NO PROBLEM AT ALL

There are successful women, some of them enormously successful, who report happy marriages and satisfying sex lives—

and no complaints from their husbands. There seem to be no clouds on their horizons, no problems they cannot solve. They all have one thing in common. They give their marriages priority over their careers.

Television personality and producer Jane Kennedy says, "Our sex life is wonderful. Bill is everything I ever wanted in a husband from the time I was a teen-ager and started dreaming about the ideal man. He is ideal as a sexual partner, a husband and a father. I couldn't want for more. In my heart I feel that my marriage works because he is the man of the house and I respect that.

"You have to be able to set aside time for you and your husband. We make very sure we have private time together. What I do when I get home at night is to turn my phones off. I don't do any business at night, because I want to spend that time with my husband. And I don't work on weekends unless I have to make an appearance somewhere.

"It is very tempting to take your work home, but I don't do that. I have cut my work down by at least forty percent since we were married two years ago.

"I do wish we had even more time together, though. Sometimes by the time the day is a wrap and Savannah is finally settled for the night, we end up with maybe half an hour to spend with each other before we both collapse."

Investment counselor Joyce Buchman, who has been married for over twenty-five years, has no complaints about her sexual life. Even though her husband was not happy about her working, her career does not seem to have interfered with their marriage in any harmful way.

"My husband was and is a very chauvinistic guy," she says. "He did not approve of my going back to work. He felt that a wife should be at home. He still believes that. But I went back to work when Jennifer was six and Jonathan was eight.

"We fought about it a lot. He gave me an ultimatum—'It's either me or work.'

"And I said, 'Joe, I love you dearly, but I'm not going to give up work.'

"There was nothing he could do. He just had to back down. And now, thirteen years later, he doesn't resent it at all. Secretly, I think he is proud of me."

Joyce was not putting her career first: she was putting herself first in this case, and that is the primary rule of survival. As she says, "It would have been awful if I had stayed a housewife. I never enjoyed it. I never had any pleasure out of it. I had no identity.

"One thing about our marriage, which is why I'm convinced it is good, is that we have always had a really good sex life. And it did not change when I went back to work. He is terrific in bed and he has always made me relax and enjoy it. It is the only area of our life that was never affected by my going back to work.

"Having enough time together was a problem until about ten years ago when we bought a house in the country for weekends. Fridays after the close of the stock market, we go there and that is our time together. We take long walks and talk. It is very relaxing. And when Sunday night comes, we feel we have shared and caught up and had a wonderful time."

Sybil Ferguson has been happily married for over thirty-five years, raised five children and founded a thriving nationwide business, Diet Center, Inc. Her priorities are firmly established.

"You cannot be totally successful in business unless you put yourself first," she says flatly, "then your husband, then your children, then your religion—and then your business. If you have things in that order, you can be totally happy.

"As you grow and develop and become successful, you have to protect the relationship with your husband so that he always feels that he comes first. I think husbands and wives should take time off every now and then and go to what I call a getaway. Our getaway is our place in the mountains on a lake.

"My husband has always been first. If he felt I was devoting too much time to the children or business, he just plain let me know it. Then we would take the weekend and go up to the lake. Roger knows very well that he comes first. That is essential.

"If you want to have a happy married relationship, there can only be one true leader in the family. I believe this very firmly. These women who are becoming self-sufficient and chauvinistic in the woman's role are not going to be able to stay married. You find that they become single women eventually.

"I always tell my Diet Center counselors, 'Make sure you make time that you can get your mind and body and feelings away from the business and make time for your husband. You need to make your husband feel important. You need to talk things over with him—even though you may be the one who makes the decisions. If you are not happy in your marriage, you can't be happy in your work,' I tell them. 'You can't give to other people. You can't be creative.'

"When Roger and I were young and had small children and money problems and all the growing pains of marriage, we used to go for rides together so that we could be alone. You just have to get out and be alone with your husband. You need to flirt with him and make him feel good about himself."

It is a prescription that has served her well. It probably also helps that Sybil's husband is almost as involved in Diet Center as she is, so that it is an interest they have together. She shares her business life as well as her personal life with her husband.

There you are. It *is* possible to have a hectic life, an erratic schedule and still have a happy marriage and a great sex life. These women are living proof of it.

I want to add one cautionary note, however, lest anyone believe that the mere absence of complaints is proof of a good relationship. Lynn Gilbert warns, "Just because someone does not complain, don't assume that everything is all right. Listen to what is not being said. Don't assume that lack of sexual activity is just because he is pressured and distracted. And don't, for that reason, decide to kind of back off and not put pressure on that part of the marriage. I suggest you double-check it out."

I believe that every woman knows deep inside whether her marriage is strong and healthy, but sometimes we tend to deny what we don't want to know. If there is little or no sexual activity in your marriage, I suggest you do something about it whether or not there are complaints. Talk about it, for starters.

Having said this, I cannot emphasize enough that while the complaint may be not enough sex, the problem is usually not sex, but priorities. In the first two or three years of a marriage, the average couple will have sex anywhere from three times a night to three times a week. Then the frequency tends to diminish—often sharply.

Studies corroborate that the importance as well as the frequency of sex lessens as the years go by. One study of 351 couples who had been married fifteen years or longer found that 300 of them were happily married. Nineteen were unhappily married. And one partner in each of the other 32 marriages was unhappy.

The happily married couples were asked what they thought was most important in maintaining a lasting and loving relationship. It was not sex. Out of fifteen items, sex was twelfth in importance for the men, fourteenth for the women. Most important for both men and women was that their spouse was their best friend. Commitment and laughter and shared goals were far more important to these happy couples than sex.

Sex is really a kind of barometer of marriage. If there is no problem, there is fair weather. The relationship is usually good. If there is a problem, expect stormy weather. It usually indicates trouble in other aspects of the relationship. When a woman gives her marriage priority, the barometric readings are usually good.

THIRTEEN

MARRIAGE IS a process. It takes time. Time to be together. Time for communication and companionship. A marriage requires tending. As John P. Marquand once said, "Marriage is a damnably serious business." It is not all wine and roses. If the relationship is not nourished, it will eventually wither. Commuter marriages are at high risk of withering.

The commuter marriage is a makeshift arrangement in which all the problems of marriage are escalated. There are no reliable statistics on the number of these marriages, but they are no longer rarities. In roughly 20 percent of Fortune 500 companies, dual-career couples present a problem. And that problem revolves around what happens when one spouse is to be transferred to another city. Since 60 percent of corporate moves involve two-career couples, the problem is no small one, particularly for women, since the wife is what corporations refer to as the "trailing spouse" in 90 percent of proposed relocations.

Some companies—roughly 30 percent of major corporations—offer relocation counseling and try to help the other spouse find a new job in the new location. For most women, however, relocation as a "trailing spouse" represents a serious career setback. A significant proportion of dual-career couples are opting for commuter marriages. They tell themselves that this is the practical way to handle the problem. This way the relocating spouse can advance his or her career and the other does not have to sacrifice his or her career. Most couples look on the separation as a short-term temporary dislocation in their marriage.

Many, possibly most, of these couples fall into the Secondary Gain Trap. They substitute something—money or advancement or power or a lover—for their original mutual goal, a good marriage in which both partners flourish. When sociologists Naomi Gerstel of the University of Massachusetts and Harriet Gross of Governors State University in Illinois interviewed 50 commuter-marriage couples, they found that the most serious problem the couples reported was that they were not there for each other. They could not give and get the emotional support that was needed and wanted. Telephone calls were not enough, no matter how long or frequent or intimate the conversations. They complained that they never had a chance to be with each other quietly, just talking or watching television or reading. Their weekends were wonderful. Exciting and sexy. Like their dating days all over again. This, the couples claimed, was the great plus in the arrangement.

On a short-term basis, this can be a plus indeed. But when the separation lasts for a year, two years or more, the euphoria of change dies down. The separation becomes a habit. Husband and wife almost invariably develop separate interests and friends. In a third of commuter marriages, one or both of the partners get involved in extramarital affairs. The weekend commute becomes a chore, a nuisance. She does not fit in his life any longer, nor he in hers. They have fallen into the Secondary Gain Trap.

There is a psychology experiment that makes the mechanics of the Secondary Gain Trap perfectly clear. In this experiment mice are put into cages that have several inches of sand on the bottom. Their food is buried under the sand. The mice can smell the food, and they dig down in the sand to get it. Each day the food is buried a little deeper until the mice have to dig three or four inches down to get at it.

Then one day the food is placed on top of the sand where the mice can see it and get at it without digging. They eat the food—and they keep on digging. These mice will dig in the sand for the rest of their lives.

Digging is not a normal mouse activity. Those mice have nothing to dig for. They will never again find any food buried in the sand. They now dig for the sake of digging, mindlessly scrabbling away in the sand. Digging has become a way of life, a reward in itself.

Let me tell you about Judy (not her real name), an extremely successful woman who—along with her husband, Adam—fell into the Secondary Gain Trap.

Judy was offered a promotion, a giant step toward her ultimate career goal. But it involved relocating to Chicago. Adam was doing too well at the bank in New York to consider moving.

Adam said, "Go for it! We'll manage. Nothing is going to come between us. It's only a three-hour plane trip. We'll see each other every weekend. And we're both so busy we hardly see each other during the week anyway."

"I'll probably be transferred back here to company headquarters in a year or so," Judy said.

"It's your big chance," Adam said. "Take it."

Judy did not fly back to New York the first weekend because she was apartment-hunting. She did not fly home the second weekend because she had found an apartment and was busy getting settled.

The third weekend she flew home. New York *was* home. Home was where Adam was. It was an hour to the airport, three hours on the plane, another hour on the bus into Manhattan. She was exhausted when she got home at midnight that Friday. But it was a great weekend. She and Adam had never been closer. And there was so much to catch up on.

Adam had planned to fly to Chicago the next weekend, but his boss asked him to take his place then at a conference. He flew to Chicago the following weekend. But not until Saturday. He picked Judy up at her office, where she was working feverishly on her first proposal for the management committee. Secretly she would have liked to have the weekend clear to work on it, but she could not tell Adam that.

It was a good weekend. She hated to say goodbye; but the minute he left, she went back to work on her proposal.

The next weekend, Judy flew to New York. Adam had the flu. "He might have let me know," she thought. "I don't need his germs." She played nurse and stocked the refrigerator and did a couple of loads of wash. She read the papers and watched television. And on Sunday, she caught the early plane back to Chicago. There was nothing she could do for Adam, and he hated having people fuss over him when he did not feel well.

She walked in the door of her Chicago apartment late that Sunday afternoon and it felt like home. A strange feeling. All of a sudden the New York apartment was Adam's and this one was hers.

Over the months Judy made friends and built up a life for herself in Chicago, but mostly she worked. And she saw Adam. Their weekends became less and less satisfactory as time went by. No matter how much they talked on the telephone, there always seemed to be an emotional distance between them when they got together.

Two years went by. Judy got a new job offer. It involved moving to Los Angeles. She accepted it without hesitation. It was a top job with top money and top perquisites. The next-to-impossible, or at least wearying, commute to New York did not enter into her decision. She wanted that job. Adam made no objection. They managed to see each other every month or so.

Then one day Adam called to say he would be in Los

Angeles that evening. They went out to dinner and he told Judy he was in love with another woman and wanted to marry her. He said he hoped she would understand. After all, it had been four years since they had lived together.

Judy understood. She had been involved with several men over these years. Nothing really serious, but, yes, she understood. If he wanted a divorce, she would not make any difficulties.

She felt hurt. Betrayed. Rejected. And relieved. They did not have a marriage. She had known it for a long time.

Judy and Adam had been deeply in love. They had been serious about their marriage. Committed to each other. Adam had agreed to the commuter marriage out of love for Judy. He wanted her to have her chance. But time and distance were their enemies. Success had come to mean more to Judy than her marriage. And another woman had come to mean more to Adam than his marriage.

If they had been living together during those four years instead of thousands of miles apart, Judy believes that they would still be married. "It is just that our lives took different directions when we were so far away from each other," she said.

A career was not really the goal that Judy had envisioned years before. Her goal had been a happy life with Adam. Yes, she wanted a challenging career, but she had always planned to stop working in a few years when they decided they were ready to have a child. This is a classic example of the Secondary Gain Trap. There is nothing wrong with changing your goal in life. It is usually a sign of development and growth. But to substitute what had been a means to an end for the goal—and without realizing what you are doing— that is sad.

Commuter marriages offer optimum opportunity for loneliness, for growing apart. They offer optimum opportunity for infidelity. They offer nothing that can strengthen a marriage.

But that won't happen with us, you may protest. We understand the perils. We have absorbed the moral of your story. We will not make those mistakes. We have talked about it from every angle and we are going to make our commuter marriage work. We will overcome the dangers.

That may be, but life does not always go according to plan. I learned this once and for all the first time I worked with rats in the psychology lab at Columbia University.

The instructor had told us to prepare for the next day's experiment by studying the section of the lab manual on handling rats. Lab rats, he warned the class, are not pets and could inflict nasty bites.

I read the manual carefully and practiced rat handling as best I could without a rat. The technique when approaching a rat is to extend your hand, flexing your fingers back so that your palm is as flat as possible. This way if a rat comes up to bite you, it cannot sink its teeth into the flesh of your palm because your hand is so rigidly extended.

Then I practiced approaching my imaginary rat from the rear and grabbing it by the back of its neck. That way the rat cannot turn around to bite you.

In the lab the next morning, I carefully extended my hand with my palm properly flattened. I put my hand behind its neck in the approved manner, ready to grab it—and another rat came up and bit me on the back of my hand!

What I learned that morning was that no matter how well prepared you may be for any dangers that confront you, you cannot always predict how things will go.

I travel all the time. My marriage could turn into a commuter—or semicommuter—marriage if I let it. But I don't. Never in my marriage have I been away for any length of time. I have been away for thousands of overnights, but I arrange my schedule so that I keep coming back home the next night.

I feel so strongly about the perils of even a semicommuter marriage that if I have to be in Los Angeles on Tuesday and Thursday, even though it does not make sense to fly back to

New York Tuesday night and then have to fly back to Los
Angeles for my Thursday engagement, I do.

I have done this literally thousands of times. I will say no
to a lecture engagement or a television appearance that would
fill in the space between a Monday when I am in New Orleans
and the Wednesday I have to be in Miami. The reason I
make such an effort to be home at least every other night is
because habit is so powerful. Most of life is habit.

Nine times out of ten when people whose marriage is in
trouble decide to live apart for a while so they can think
things over quietly, they never get back together. They had
worked out who does the laundry and who vacuums and
who takes the car to be serviced. When they interrupt these
habits and the husband discovers that he likes frozen dinners and takeout food and that it is easy to drop his laundry
off at the Laundromat in the morning and that he can
hire a maid service to dig him out from under every couple of weeks, and she finds that she is not nervous about
being alone at night ever since she got the dog and the dog
is much easier to get along with than her husband and it is
really very nice to come home from work and flop on the
couch instead of starting dinner—well, this is the way marriages unravel.

Milt has many things to fill his time with on the nights I'm
not home. He has friends with whom he plays squash and
poker. Lately he has become interested in astronomy. And
he always has professional reading to do. But I don't want
him to reach a point where he has worked out a certain
amount of comfort for himself without me, worked out a
night every week when he does this or that. I don't want him
to form new habits that don't include me. This way he is
always happy to have me come home. He says it is more fun
when I am there, and I want to keep it that way. I never
want him to get used to being without me.

I make a point of keeping in touch while I am away. I call
him every day to share what has gone on in my life and ask
him how his day has been. My phone bills are exorbitant, but

every minute I spend talking with Milt while I'm away is time and money well spent. We don't have a chance to get out of touch with each other or form new habits.

There are some commuter marriages that I consider justified, but they are special situations. I mentioned one in Chapter Six, where I suggested that a six-month commuter marriage might solve problems connected with a husband's relocation. The key here is the short and definitely limited period of time. A good marriage should not be threatened by six months of partial separation.

And then there are situations where a commuter marriage is forced upon a couple. In the military, for instance. There are thousands and thousands of military marriages that have survived the stresses and perils of being apart. An important factor in these marriages is that the separations are caused by maneuvers or sea duty or military actions, situations in which the husband (or wife) does not establish a separate home. He or she usually lives in barracks or on board ship or submarine in conditions that make home and spouse extremely desirable. These are really not commuter marriages, since they are the result of duty rather than choice.

Barbara Kelley and her husband, Marine Corps Commandant P. X. Kelley, have been happily married for thirty-six years, despite frequent long separations. Their secret has been trust and constant communication.

"We've had such a life of upheaval and separation," Barbara told interviewer Diana McLellan in *The Washingtonian*. "We moved thirty-five times in thirty-two years. The first forty-eight months of our marriage, we were separated for forty of them. When P. X. was in Vietnam—for two separate one-year stretches—we both wrote each other every day. There is something about writing that is even more personal, more special and more intimate than speech."

Another kind of commuter marriage that I consider justified is that of a husband and wife who have been married for a long time and have a mutually rewarding relationship.

Again, I am thinking about marriages like Ambassador Jeane Kirkpatrick's when she was at the United Nations.

"Much of my United Nations period I was away from home and apart from my husband," Ambassador Kirkpatrick said. "We did an awful lot of talking on the telephone. We always spoke at least once a day to each other, and we got together on weekends most of the time.

"Sometimes I grew very discouraged and I would come home and say I was ready to quit. He would sort of dust me off and send me back into the fray. He thought it was an important job for me to do, and he gave me tremendous encouragement.

"I missed him and I didn't enjoy being away from him, but I was so incredibly busy, almost too busy to be lonely. I found it somewhat oppressive.

"I would not myself recommend anybody try to live that way or do that kind of job if her children are young. There is simply no time in that kind of job to do anything else but that job. I also would not have wanted to try it if I had been married less than the twenty-six years we had been married at that time. The support of a secure husband and a secure relationship is vital."

When it comes to making the case against long separations in marriage, I do not think anyone could put it better than Julie Nixon Eisenhower, who was separated from her husband for long periods in the first years of their marriage.

"We were separated too much during the early years of our marriage. It was very bad. It was difficult for us during the Presidential years with David being in the Navy. He was with the Sixth Fleet for three years, and then he was in law school for three years. At that time I was an editor for the Curtis Publishing Company at its headquarters in Indianapolis. I would fly out to Indianapolis for two days a week and work from home during the rest of the time. We really didn't have a normal married life until David finished law school and we moved to California in 1977, and then Jenny was born in 1978.

"Even now we have so little time for ourselves, it's terrible. We like to go out by ourselves for dinner and just relax and talk, and then we come home and sit together and read, or maybe we rent a movie or just have a very quiet time.

"Just recently we were separated much too much when we were promoting our books [Julie's biography of her mother, Pat Nixon, and David's biography of his grandfather, President Dwight D. Eisenhower]. We hated that.

"You have to build a life together," Julie said earnestly. "It is good to have separate interests, but you have to have time together. When two people are leading two high-powered lives and traveling in separate directions, it can really cause strains."

FOURTEEN

"I don't have a friend, actually."

"I can't spend the time to develop a friendship."

"I have no friends."

"I did have some friends, but I lost them."

ONE OF the saddest trade-offs made by successful women is friendship. Many of them do not have the time to invest in friendship. Friendships must be fed, must be nurtured. And this takes time. They may have scores of acquaintances, be on friendly terms with business associates and professional colleagues, but they have no real friends.

"A person has to make choices," says Susan Petersen, president of Ballantine–Del Rey–Fawcett Books. "In my case I gave up friendship. I don't go home and cook dinner for five of my closest friends. I have no time to socialize. It is either business or my family. That's it."

Chris Boe Voran says, "I didn't have time to make friends when I was working. I did have some friends, but I lost them from constantly cancelling dinner dates or theater arrangements or weekend trips. My friends quickly realized that I was one of the more untrustworthy people in terms of being able to keep social engagements, because as a young lawyer—

147

and law is a service business—I was very much at the whim of the client and of the partners for whom I worked."

"I have no friends," says retailer Lana Jane Lewis-Brent. "I simply don't have the time. My first priority is running the business."

Gillian Sorensen says, "I don't have time for friends. That has had to go. There just isn't time."

Jane Kennedy says, "Because of my schedule, it is very difficult to have a relationship with a friend, because I can never see them. I can't spend the time to develop a friendship. I think friendships are special. I have a lot of associates, but I don't think I could say that I have friends."

"One of the trade-offs I made was that I had very little time to be with people whom I cared about," says Felice Schwartz, founder of Catalyst. "Therefore I didn't develop friendships the way I would have liked."

Actress Lynn Redgrave told me, "I can't say that I have any close friends. I don't have a friend, actually. I do have lots of chums. If I call them up or they come around or we go to their house, I have lots of fun and laughs, but I don't have a close friend. When I was younger and single, I certainly did have women friends. We used to call each other up and pour our hearts out over the telephone for an hour and a half. I don't have the sort of life now when I can do that."

Then there are the women who dearly want friends, who do the best they can to hold on to old friends. Time is their enemy. Nevertheless, they manage somehow to hold on to old friends.

When I asked Joan Rivers about friends, she said, "Oh, they've gone by the board. We just don't make new friends. There is no time to be social. We have very few friends and the ones we have are really old friends."

"Friends are very hard to work into my life, although they are so important," said Marilyn Moore. "I have had one close friend since high school, but I never have enough time to spend with her. We have lunch together once a week or every other week. Once in a while we will have breakfast together on a Saturday."

"I gave up a lot of friends when I went to work," Joyce Buchman said. "I had a lot of women friends who just did not understand. I would call them and they would ask why I couldn't have lunch and all that. They just couldn't understand. I miss them.

"I do have one friend who does not work. She lives right across the street. I get to see her often, and our kids are good friends. Her husband is a lawyer, just as my husband is, so we are very close and we are best friends. We spend holidays together with both our families. We kind of don't need a lot of other people."

Nancy Evans said, "I don't get together with my friends very often. Here is how pathetic it is: my closest friend and I have a standing lunch date once a month. We arranged this because I realized that if we didn't, months could go by and we might not see each other."

In dozens of surveys, men have reported that their best friend is their wife. A woman's best friend may be her husband—mine is—but more often it is another woman. This is not a reflection upon a woman's relationship with her husband. She looks upon him as her lover and partner in life, but not as a friend. Letty Cottin Pogrebin, a founding editor of *Ms.* magazine and author of a recent book on friendship, says that "Most women will say that their husband is their best friend, but it's not true. They are not telling their husband a whole lot of things that they are telling their women friends."

Friends actually seem to be more necessary to women than to men. They certainly fill different roles for women than for men. Men play golf with, have drinks with, talk business with, swap gossip with the men they consider their friends. Once in a blue moon, a man will confide in a friend, admit to being worried about his children or his health. But only once in a blue moon.

Women also play golf with, have drinks with, talk business

with and swap gossip with their women friends. But they do more. Women talk to, confide in, ask advice from, give advice to, share their lives with their women friends. Female friendships tend to be deeper, more caring, more involved than male friendships. And women will make serious efforts to develop friendships.

Karen Nussbaum says, "I had to decide that I would carve out special time for friends. I had to make a real change in my life to do this.

"We moved to Cleveland, and after a few years I found that my friends had moved away. All of a sudden I did not have anyone to call to do something with. My life had really changed. Outside of work, it largely revolved around the children. I wanted friendships. I need other women to talk with.

"I told my husband I needed new friends and needed to have time to spend with them. He understood. When I say, 'I'd really like to do this with a friend tonight,' he says, 'Okay.' He is sad about it, though, because it is one night that we might have been together.

"I can only see friends on nights when he will be home to be with the children. It is hard, but I think that a lot of things that are difficult right now, because our children are so young, will be different once they are a little older."

Many very highly successful women, I discovered, make a point of cultivating friendships no matter what the demands upon their time. They have chosen to invest precious time in building and strengthening friendships. They understand just how important friends are to the quality of their lives.

Barbara Walters, for one, cannot imagine life without friends, and she works to keep her friendships alive. "I would be lost without my friends," Barbara told me. "I know some very successful women who really don't have time for friendship. I do, but I do a lot of it on the telephone.

"I think it is easier if you are not married; then you have more time for your women friends. What I miss is the long lunches with them, but I keep in touch, even if sometimes it is just a long Sunday telephone conversation. I could not get along without friends, and I have never had to give them up."

"Friends and family are the two most important ingredients for a happy life," says Julie Nixon Eisenhower. "Keeping up with my friends means everything to me. I have a lot of friends that don't live in this area, but I see them as often as I can. They come to visit, and I go to visit them with my children. We talk on the phone often.

"I think women tend to have wonderful friendships that they really cultivate. It does take time, but it gives you so much in return."

"I make time for friends," Jacqueline Leo says. "I'm in the magazine business. You can't live in a vacuum and edit a magazine. We really have a family of friends, most of us relatively new parents. We all make our weekends revolve around the children to some extent, although we certainly have our share of dinner parties on a Saturday night.

"Friends are important. My friends are my best resources in terms of my emotional jolts."

"I have a lot of close friends and I spend a lot of time with them," says novelist Sally Quinn. "I hang out with my friends. I talk to them on the phone. I see them on weekends. I really like to keep in touch with them. Now that I am working at home, I have more time for them than I did before. Like yesterday—I sat with my son for two hours while he watched *Sesame Street* and I talked to friends on the phone."

"It is easy for the pace of events to crowd out what is important to the First Lady as a person," Nancy Reagan told a group of newspaper publishers. "It is very important that a First Lady not let her old friendships wither. And that can happen, because friends think you are so busy that they feel they should not intrude.

"I am a big believer that you have to nourish any relationship. I am still very much a part of my friends' lives and they are very much a part of my life. You have heard a lot about my trusty telephone, but I don't think people realize that it is my lifeline to friends, some of whom I have known for thirty-five or forty years. I think that a First Lady who does not have this source of strength and comfort can lose perspective and become isolated."

Women face hard choices when it comes to friends. And there seems to be an increasing tendency for women to believe that they do not and cannot have time for friends because of the energy and time demanded by their careers and families. This is probably true in a great many cases, but I would like to quote what Professor Rita Levi-Montalcini, co-winner of the 1986 Nobel Prize for medicine and a very wise woman, has to say about success and friendship.

"It is very dangerous," Dr. Levi-Montalcini says, "especially for young people, to live in a state of obsession, always worried about career or success. It is egocentric. We must keep our minds open to the problems of the larger society. The best of life is friendship—what you can do for the other."

One thing every woman should know about friends is that they are good for you. They not only enrich your life, they are a bulwark against stress, as I explain in the following chapter. Dr. Joel Bloch, a clinical psychologist who has interviewed some two thousand people on friendship, says, "I don't consider friendship an optional relationship. It is an important relationship that helps a person to function fully."

I agree wholeheartedly with Dr. Bloch—even though, as I wrote in an earlier chapter, I am one of those women who found that the demands of career and family left no time for friends.

FIFTEEN

PRESSURES, PRESSURES, pressures! The working wife's life—far more than her husband's—is full of pressure. Career pressure, marriage pressure, child-care pressure, family pressure. Sexual, mental, emotional and physical pressures. She tries to meet all the demands put upon her, but there come times when enough is enough, when enough is too much. Fatigue sets in. Guilt. Resentment. The sun no longer shines. This is stress. This is when trying to have it all or even just part of it threatens to overwhelm the working woman.

In the last few years, a significant number of successful young women have complained of "burnout" and given up their careers and professions to stay home and take care of the children. At the same time, hundreds of thousands of successful women are juggling career, marriage and children and thriving on the challenge.

What is the difference between these two groups?

The major difference is that many of the women who complain of burnout have unconsciously reordered their priorities. They no longer crave career success. It is as simple as that. However, when they leave their jobs, they cite burnout as the reason, because they truly believe they have become stressed to the point of ineffectiveness. Burned out.

What has really happened is that they have lost what Dr. Estelle Ramey of Georgetown University Medical School calls "the motive force." A woman can be well rested and still wake up every morning feeling exhausted. "This," says Dr. Ramey, "is because the perception of your state of well-being resides in the brain. And this perception can be altered by things other than your physical state. Energy depends on the motive force. Women can continue for extraordinary lengths of time if the motivation and rewards are great enough," she says.

If what a woman really wants is to be home with her children, to be a mother and a homemaker, the power and money and status that accrue to a successful working woman will never be sufficient reward for her. The career woman who has unconsciously decided that she would rather be at home becomes divided and conflicted about what she is doing. This creates a high level of anxiety.

And anxiety, explains Dr. Helen De Rosis, clinical associate professor of psychiatry at New York University School of Medicine, can wear you out. "When you put yourself wholeheartedly into something," she says, "energy grows. It seems inexhaustible. If, on the other hand, you are divided and conflicted about what you are doing, you create anxiety. And the amount of physical and emotional energy consumed by anxiety is exorbitant."

These women who have given up their careers are doing the right thing—for the wrong reason. They are listening to their inner self and choosing the way of life they really want without understanding what they are doing or why. And many of them pay a price for this ignorance. Despite the satisfaction they feel once they have made their choice, they tend to feel guilty, because they feel that they are not using their full potential. They feel as if they have cheated themselves. Some even feel that they have failed. And of course, this is not true.

Every woman who feels overstressed should take time to reconsider her goals. What are your real priorities? Take time to do a new Goal Analysis (see Chapter Five). If the new Goal Analysis shows that what you really want to do in life is be a wife and mother, then this will be the best of all worlds for you. You should let yourself enjoy it without guilt. Raising a child to be a healthy, happy, reasonable and responsible human being certainly ranks high among life's achievements. There is no reason for guilt if this is your choice.

Then there is the woman whose career means everything to her—or almost. She may put her marriage ahead of her career, but she would never in the world consider giving up her career to stay home and keep house.

But suddenly everything is just too much. The new baby keeps her up most of the night. The three-year-old has a severe case of sibling rivalry and seems to have regressed to Terrible Twohood. Her husband complains about the incessant upset in the household and feels neglected. The housekeeper says two children are too many and gives notice. Her boss sends her a stinging memo criticizing her sales plan for the next quarter.

Who needs it? She decides to resign and take over the reins at home.

This woman too claims to be burned out. She is not. What she is is temporarily overstressed. She loves her work, thrives on the challenges, has always looked forward to going back to work after the weekend. Does she really want to stay at home?

No! If she does a new Goal Analysis, it will show that her goals have not changed. She still wants to succeed in her field, although her definition of success may be higher now than it used to be. If this woman gives up her work to stay home, there is every chance that she will regret her decision within a year. Probably within a week.

What I can tell these women is that the particular crisis or stress-filled period will pass. It is temporary. Nothing ever lasts forever.

The baby will start sleeping through the night. The three-year-old will adjust. You will find another housekeeper. Yes, it is hard on your husband, but probably not as hard as it is on you. He must understand that this is temporary stress, not a long-term lifestyle, and that there is a lot he can do to help you survive these weeks or months. As for your boss, well, now that you have his input, you will probably come up with an even better sales plan.

But right now you need first aid. Get all the help you can. Cut whatever corners you can. Make whatever compromises you must. If necessary, break the budget or float a loan to pay for extra help until you are over the hump. Do whatever you can to hang in there. If you resign and focus your energies on running the household, you may find that you have jumped from the frying pan into a bonfire.

"Stress is seen as an ailment that can be caught at work and not at home," says Dr. Grace Baruch, program director of the Wellesley College Center for Research on Women. Not so, she emphasizes. The fact is that home and family tend to be significantly more stressful than work.

Your job may be your safety valve—a stress-alleviator rather than a stress-spawner. It is not unusual for women to bounce out of the house on Monday morning feeling, "Thank God it's Monday" as they escape back to work, where life is so much simpler and more straightforward, where the goals are clear and the rewards are tangible. As one woman said (and I wish I knew her), "A job is to a woman as a wife is to a man—the ultimate stress buffer."

For every burnt-out case, as I said earlier, there are hundreds of thousands who are subject to equal amounts of stress, who seem to sail through everything from sick children to corporate takeovers. They get tired. They may get crotchety. But they manage.

Their secret? They know how to cope with stress.

Stress is all in your head—at the beginning. The stress response starts in the hypothalamus, a pea-sized area of the brain. When you encounter a stressful situation, the hypothalamus causes the adrenal glands to release more adrenaline and glucocorticoids into the bloodstream. The adrenaline gives you the energy to cope with whatever is causing you stress. It makes your heart beat faster, makes you breathe faster and increases your blood pressure.

The glucocorticoids travel through your bloodstream back to the brain to a structure called the hippocampus. Depending on the glucocorticoid level, the hippocampus signals the hypothalamus. The more glucocorticoids in the blood, the stronger the signal. This new stress alarm causes the hypothalamus to signal the adrenal glands again. And so it goes.

If it is a short-term stress situation—the switchboard cuts you off in the middle of an important call; your seven-year-old notifies you he needs a Halloween costume for school tomorrow morning; you and your husband argue about whether you really have to go to his mother's for supper Sunday night—the adrenaline and glucocorticoid levels subside fairly rapidly once the stress situation is over.

Basically, stress is a matter of how you react to a situation. If you can take something like the switchboard cutting you off in the middle of an important call in your stride, you are not going to feel particularly stressed. But if you react as if it were a matter of life and death, if you keep on stewing about it and cursing the switchboard operator and worrying that you have lost a commission just because the call was cut off, your stress response is going to stay high for a long time.

Researchers working with rats have found that high levels of adrenaline and glucocorticoids over a long period of time result in brain damage. And in rats, the damage is permanent. The effect of prolonged high stress in humans appears to be less debilitating. But given my druthers, I would prefer to keep my stress situations short and sweet.

Stress *can* be sweet. We thrive on appropriate amounts of stress. No vitamin can perk you up the way stress can. A *Wall*

Street Journal survey of women executives revealed that 75 percent of them enjoyed job-related stress. It was a high for them, not a source of anxiety. This bears out what Dr. Hans Selye, the father of stress research, always said: a certain amount of stress is good for you. Stress is destructive only when it gets out of control, when you are no longer in charge.

An imaginative experiment involving rats and their need for a degree of control over their lives was carried out by endocrinologist Estelle Ramey. Rats were trained to perform certain tasks. When they succeeded, they got a food treat. When they failed, they got an electric shock. The rats soon learned what they had to do in order to get treats and avoid shocks. They were in control of this part of their lives.

Then Dr. Ramey changed the rules. When a rat succeeded, sometimes it got a treat and sometimes it got a shock. Now the rat did not know what the consequences of its actions would be. It could no longer control that sector of its life. It was completely unpredictable.

The result? The rats began to bleed internally and died very soon after.

"If rats, with their pin brains, respond that way to helpless frustration," Dr. Ramey says, "it is not hard to understand what it can do to a woman."

How do you stay in control? The prescription is very simple. You do something. You act. "Movement is built into the system as an appropriate response to stress," Dr. Ramey says. "When you are tense, your capillaries constrict and can't deliver blood to muscles and cells." Exercise will relax your capillaries and restore the normal flow of blood.

There are few people who know more about stress than British Prime Minister Margaret Thatcher. "The burden is greater than most people realize," she says. "Sometimes you just have to take your mind off it.

"What do you do? You go for a walk. It does not matter if it is raining or blowing. You get the air into your lungs.

And sometimes I read late at night to take things out of my mind and put something else in."

Evelyn Handler, president of Brandeis University, agrees. "Exercise," she says. "And when you can't, move. I never sit at my desk for more than an hour."

"Exercise is the only answer," confirms Dorothy Brunson, president of Brunson Communications. "I leave the office and walk around the block as many times as I need to."

I have found that exercise works well for me. If I have a stress overload and start snapping at people, I get out my jump rope, and in five minutes I feel a lot better. What helps most of all is getting out to the farm with Milt and working outside—weeding the garden, pruning trees, mowing, raking, whatever. I find that working up a sweat is a wonderful antidote for stress.

Pat Collins retreats into what she calls "the trivial"—and others might consider a frenzy of activity—when things get to be too much.

"I turn to domestic planning," Pat says. "I make up the menus and lists of what has to go to the cleaners and what birthdays are coming up and who gets what gift and who's in the car pool and which children can come in to play after school. It is boring, but it is easy to do and it is relaxing.

"I make snap decisions and they are often wrong, but at least I've made the decision. My husband is more of a deep thinker. He ponders the benefits of Kevin Warble's birthday party, while I simply say yes and here's what Andrew is wearing and this is what he is taking as a present and here is the check for it and here is the card and make sure Andrew signs it.

"And I clean closets. There is something very rewarding about cleaning closets. When you've finished, you have something to show for it.

"I actually relish these chores. There is something very soothing about trivial tasks. They have to be done, so you can do them without feeling guilty that you are not doing something very important. And if you don't put mozzarella cheese on the shopping list, no one is going to shoot you. Chores are a nice escape hatch from the hectic part of my life."

Many of the successful women I talked with told me they handled stress by preventive planning. Mary Cunningham's background as a strategic planner (she was vice president for strategic planning at the Bendix Corporation and later vice president for strategic planning and project development at Seagram's) has helped her keep destructive stress at bay despite a hectic life.

"As a strategic planner," she says, "you spend a great deal of time in the corporate world setting goals, identifying where you want to go, how you want to get from here to there, prioritizing what you want to accomplish, setting in motion plans of action that will allow you to achieve those goals. You develop contingency plans as well, because things do not always play out the way you thought they would.

"These are the same skills you need in your personal life. I sit down and take stock about every three months. I ask myself how am I doing on the things that matter to me.

"How am I in terms of my marriage? Am I a good partner and wife?

"What kind of mother am I being?

"How good is this career? Am I really contributing to my clients what they deserve?

"How about my health?

"I look at these as goals that need to be achieved. At any given moment, I could say that one is being sacrificed for another, but I don't let that go on for more than two or three days. It is a balancing act. Everyone has her own point of equilibrium, and that is defined by knowing yourself well enough to know what the components of your equilibrium are. For me, they are marriage, motherhood, career and good health. Preserving my health doesn't matter as much as the others. It is the one that drops to the bottom every time."

Faye Wattleton, president of Planned Parenthood, also employs preventive planning to keep stress at bay. Her weekends are kept free for herself, her daughter and her friends. "It is important to set priorities. There is only so much you can handle. It is very easy to get caught up in other people's demands. You have to remember that nurturing yourself is just as important."

Faye makes time for herself during the week by walking to work. She also schedules time alone just the way she schedules meetings. "And if things really get too much for me, I will go away for the weekend."

Jane Kennedy also makes a point of setting aside time for herself—time away from her work, from her husband, from her baby. "You have to be able to set aside time for yourself just so you can think things through, so you can have your priorities straight and know what you want to do. It is easy to just go through the routine and do what needs to be done. You also have to be able to decide what you want to do."

The kind and amount of time successful women need to avoid destructive stress varies from individual to individual. Helen Gurley Brown, for instance, really does not feel right unless she is rather highly stressed. On weekends, when most working women relax, she works.

"My husband never sees me on weekends except at meals," Helen says. "I cook our meals over the weekends, but the rest of the time I work hard on *Cosmo*. I cannot do heavy thinking during the week. I'm just too busy working with the staff and being a good boss. So on weekends, I simply have to do what I do: WORK!"

In her way, this is Helen's time for herself. She is doing what she wants to do. She would feel more stressed if she felt that her weekends had to be devoted to entertaining or gallery hopping or long walks or whatever.

Some women make drastic changes in their lives to avoid heavy stress. "One of the reasons I left my position as president of production at Twentieth Century–Fox," Sherry Lansing says, "was because I wanted more time for myself. At Fox, it was seven-day weeks and eighteen-hour days. It became literally impossible to have a balanced life, and I didn't want that.

"I want a great job and I also want a great personal life. Today, as an independent producer, I have both seventy-five percent of the time. I usually get to the office at nine and I leave around six, sometimes seven. Then I go out to dinner and a movie, or I stay home and read, or I play tennis—do whatever I feel like. The twenty-five percent of the year when I am producing a film, my life is all work. But I know it will be over in three months and that lets me enjoy it."

One of the greatest stressors on women is guilt. Guilt that they are not spending enough time with their children, that they are taking time from their family for work, that their work is suffering because of the time and energy they put into their marriage and family. Lois Wyse, advertising agency head and writer, advises women to fight a conscious battle against being overcome by guilt.

"I think that if there was only one thing I could say to a woman, it would be to understand that you cannot be guilt-free. If you feel guilty, that is just part of life. There is no woman who can work and raise children and not feel guilty. You know that when you are at home, you should be at work. And when you are at work, you should be at home. You feel that you are never in the right place at the right time, and so there is bound to be guilt."

My daughter, Lisa, has the same attitude. She says, "I have come to feel that no matter what is it that I am feeling guilty about at the moment, if I didn't have that to feel guilty about, I would feel guilty about something else. Guilt is just part of life."

Just knowing this alleviates some of the stress. You are no different from hundreds of thousands of other working wives and mothers. You are doing your best. There is no need to feel guilty. And if you do, just ask yourself this: "Does my husband feel guilty?" Nine hundred ninety-nine times out of a thousand, you know the answer is "No!" And these are very generous odds. So, if he can work and not be consumed with guilt over whether he is devoting enough time to you, enough time to the children, why should you? Just remember that you are a role model for your children, and a working mother is probably the most helpful role model they can have these days.

Successful women also warn against turning to destructive remedies for coping with stress. These include food binges, drugs, alcohol and smoking. These crutches may alleviate stress for the moment, but their long-term effect is increased stress—physical, mental and emotional.

"When I go to a meeting," says Lynn Gilbert, "I can tell how good everyone's business is by whether or not they have gained weight. If the women are fat, then business has been slow."

When stress reaches the overload point, some women cry. In private. My daughter, Lisa, is one of them. "I cry a lot," she told me. "When things get too much for me, I go to the bedroom and close the door and cry. It really seems to help."

Interestingly enough, crying truly is an effective stress-dispeller. One study, headed by William Frey, a biochemist at St. Paul–Ramsey Medical Center in St. Paul, Minnesota, tested the tears of 43 women, aged seventeen to thirty-eight, and found that they contain stress-related hormones, which leads him to believe that crying is a way of physically purging stress from the body. Other scientists have found that stress-induced tears have a different chemical composition from tears produced by a speck in the eye or other physical eye irritation.

Almost all successful women turn to friends or family when they are stressed. Barbara Hendricks, the soprano, turns to her husband, who is also her manager. "When I am feeling particularly stressed, I like to blame my husband. If I feel that I have too many concerts in a certain period of time and have much too much to learn, well, he is a very close target. But we are always able to talk about it, and he is the first one to say, 'All right, now. Then that has to go and this has to go. You stay home for a while.'

"I remember when I made my debut in *Romeo et Juliette* at the Paris Opera, my son was just six months old and I was breast-feeding him. My husband said, 'Stop it. You are exhausted.' And he was right. Just one week after I stopped breast-feeding, all of a sudden I could hold the high C at the end of the aria."

Betty Ann Davis (not her real name), head of a large fashion house, finds that her friends help her live through stress situations. "When fabrics don't arrive on time or the fashion press is snotty about a collection, I feel like jumping out the window. But I don't. I get on the telephone to my friends. I dump it all on them. I will spend hours on the phone. And it helps. It really does. I get it all talked out of my system and then I am ready to go again.

"And I do the same for my friends. I'm always there for them. I always will be. I don't know what I would do without them."

Keeping a sense of perspective may be the most effective stress-reliever of all. It takes time and experience to develop a perspective on your life and your work, but it is a goal to work toward. Lois Wyse put it very well when she said, "I think when you get to a certain point in your life, you have a sense of what is important and what is not. And I think most women who work come to that point faster than women who have never worked. The reason is that they have many more decisions to make and they realize that everything is not overwhelming. Particularly in business.

"If you ever go back and look through your datebook and see what you were doing a year ago, you see what looked so important to you a year ago and now it is just totally forgotten. Therefore the things that are very important to you, that are overwhelming today, somehow or other in another year they will be forgotten.

"If you just take this same attitude into your personal life and realize that there is nothing that matters except the two of you and the value of the time you spend together and what you can give each other in terms of emotional support, well, that is really what life is about."

Sixteen

No DOUBT about it, money is power. It used to be that men wielded money as their power weapon and women used sex as theirs. This is no longer universally true. With increasing numbers of men blaming their ambitious working wives for their impotence, the withholding of sex has become as much a male weapon as a female one. And with women brandishing their earnings as a symbol of independence, sending the message "I can get along without you very well," money has become part of the female arsenal. Most marital fights are about money—or so it seems. The truth is that what money fights are about is power.

In the course of interviewing highly successful women, I discovered that money and power are rarely issues in their marriages, although when they are, they are blockbuster issues. What surprised me most was the cavalier—or possibly simply old-fashioned—attitude toward money demonstrated by some successful women.

Take Helen Gurley Brown, for example. This staunch believer that women can do anything and everything says, "My paycheck is just sent over to my husband's office every week. I never even look at it. He makes more money than I do, and besides, he is really scrupulously trustable."

Joan Rivers is another. "Money was always very easy between us," Joan says. "I always let Edgar handle it. He did all the investments. We discussed everything, but I really took his word for things. I know how much I'm worth, but I really don't give a damn. I would if there was no money. Then I'd be saying, 'Where did it all go?' I don't have much money sense. I think letting him handle it, I came out better."

"I just hand all the money I earn over to my husband," says Joyce Buchman, the investment counselor. "He is very successful and very generous. I have never had to really think about money. I buy all my own clothes and charge whatever I want to charge. I don't go out and buy jewelry and furs. I'm not a spoiled brat. If I want to make a major purchase, I always say, 'I need a fur jacket,' for example, and then he goes with me, the way we used to when we first got married. We don't have any money problems."

Not every woman is as blithe as these three about handing over her earnings to her husband. Most share financial obligations with their husbands according to fairly informal formulas they have worked out between them.

"We put our money into one pot and we sort of both spend whatever we want to," says Karol Emmerich. "It works out all right. When we made a lot less money, eight or nine years ago, it was more difficult. We had some fights then about money, but not anymore. Now that there is more than either of us spend, it is very simple. We just do what we want to do."

"We have a marriage that is very free of conflict over money," says Karen Nussbaum. "It is not really an issue for us. Earning more money is not a sign of success or a status symbol that we consider important or a measure of our importance in our own work. We are fortunate in that we both work for

organizations that we care very much about. I feel that we
are very lucky people.

"We don't have any of the frills, but we don't really feel
we are missing out on anything. I wouldn't mind having
someone come in to do the housework if we had more money.
But basically, we have all we need."

Jun Kanai, the Japanese fashion representative, says, "I
pay the bills. I like to know what is going on, but I will not
spend any money unless that is what my husband wants to
do. And he has the final say if we have a disagreement. That
is my Japanese upbringing."

"My husband and I seldom disagree on money," says Barbara Hendricks. "Neither of us came from a wealthy family.
The money we have, we made. When we were first married,
my husband would always ask my permission to buy a shirt
or a tie. He would say, 'I want to buy this. What do you think?
Come and look at it.' I did the same thing. I would say, 'I
saw a gown that I could use for recitals. What do you think?'
We don't do that anymore.

"We have always discussed any big purchase, though. We
say, 'If we buy this, where is it going to put us?' Our income
is not steady. He is an agent and manager for musicians and
singers. And my work schedule is erratic. I may work for two
months and then not work for a month. So when we face a
big purchase, we have to say, 'Where is this going to leave
us in six months?' But it is really no problem. Neither one
of us is the kind to live above our means. As a matter of fact,
before the children came along, we always lived below our
means."

"We don't have problems about money, although we have
other problems," says Marilyn Moore. "We decided before
we got married—and this was one of the very good things
we did—exactly how we were going to handle money. At that
time we were making close to the same amount. We decided
to split things fifty–fifty and we still do, although I am, of
course, responsible for feeding and clothing my children from
my first marriage. But everything else is fifty–fifty."

Sybil Ferguson and her husband, Roger, have never had any problems handling money either.

"I always handled the money in the early days of our marriage when we really didn't have any," Sybil says. "I paid the bills. And if I wanted a new dress or a lamp for the living room, I went out and got a job to pay for it. I sold encyclopedias. I sold memberships to the country club. I did a lot of things like that so I had extra money.

"Then as I began to open Diet Centers and make money, Rog was doing well too. In 1976, he sold his farm for over a million dollars and then he said, 'Sybil, what do you want to do with this money? You can put it in the bank and live off the interest for the rest of your life. You can take trips to Europe, buy all the clothes you want, remodel the house, buy a new house, any number of things. Or,' he said, 'you can put it into Diet Centers.'

"And I said, 'I'd love to put it into Diet Centers. I know that we have a service that will help people.' So we invested that money in the business and were able to move forward.

"We have always worked together. In the beginning, whenever I wanted to set up a new Diet Center, Rog would show me where the money was and say, 'Now, if you do this, you will have to give this up. What do you want to do?' And we would talk it out.

Many couples find that they have absolutely different attitudes toward money, but nevertheless money is not a cause of dissension. They respect each other's attitudes.

"My Yankee frugality sometimes gets in the way," says Pat Collins. "Joe would never dream of buying anything extravagant for himself, but when he sees something for me, he doesn't even think about money. When he was in London once, he bought a beautiful peignoir and nightgown for me from Janet Regers. It must have cost at least six hundred dollars, because nothing at Janet Regers is much less. When he brought it home, I feigned delight, but all the time I was thinking, 'Oh, what I could have done with six hundred dol-

lars!' But Joe just wanted to get me something wonderful
that he knew I would never buy for myself. I've never worn
it. It is still there. I ought to wear it. After all, what am I
saving it for? Anyway, Joe will do that kind of thing where
it would never occur to me. Never! Ever!

"A couple of years ago, Joe wanted to take the whole family—his kids, our kids—to London for Christmas. I looked
at him and said, 'Are you crazy? Do you know what that is
going to cost?'

"And Joe said, 'Okay, so we won't go to London for Christmas. We'll go out and buy some plum pudding and hire some
carolers. You're right; I was wrong,' he said. And that was
the end of that.

"Our accountant handles our money. This is the best way
to save a marriage—having a third party handle your money.
Our accountant is very good and conservative. If we are
thinking of a big purchase, he will tell us whether we should
do it or not. And then Joe and I talk and decide whether it
is really a good thing to do."

Linda Grant and her husband also have an accountant
handle their money. "He sends us an allowance," Linda says,
"so all the emotion has been removed. The accountant pays
the bills.

"I feel fortunate that when I wanted to take off to stay
home with our son, my husband's career was really in full
swing. He is probably at the peak of his earning power. We
have not had to make sacrifices. And money has not been a
problem."

All of these women agree that each partner should have
money of his or her own that can be spent without having
to account for it. I call this MOMO—Money Of My Own. I
have always advised couples to establish MOMO accounts, no
matter how much or how little money is available.

Milt and I have always had MOMOs. When we were first
married, we allowed ourselves each fifty cents a week. I usually squandered mine on chocolate bars. Now that we don't
have to watch our pennies, we still have MOMO accounts.

They make life much more fun. A couple of years ago, I dipped into mine and bought Milt a bright red sports car for his birthday.

Another time, it must have been nearly twenty years ago, I arranged for him to have two squash lessons with Hashim Khan, something that meant even more at the time to Milt than that red sports car did later on. Milt then played squash two and three times a week and studied the game the way some men study the stock market. He was always wrapped around a book called *Squash Rackets: The Khan Game* by Hashim Khan, then the world's most famous squash player.

I discovered that Hashim Khan was teaching in Detroit. Without telling Milt, I accepted a lecture engagement in Detroit for a Saturday, something I seldom do because weekends are strictly family time, and I called Hashim Khan to ask if he would give Milt two lessons during that weekend. He agreed.

When I told Milt I had a weekend lecture, he was mildly annoyed but agreed to go to Detroit to keep me company. The whole surprise worked out wonderfully. This was something Milt would never have done for himself, and I loved being able to do it for him.

Milt has used his MOMO account to buy me wonderful presents too. One time he came home with a huge hat box full of mink pelts. He had wanted to buy me a fur coat, but he did not want to risk choosing a style I might not like. Instead, he gave me the pelts to have made into any style I wanted. A couple of years ago, he surprised me with a tractor of my own for the farm.

But we don't usually spend our MOMO accounts on each other. I still buy chocolates with mine. I feel they are such a wicked indulgence they should not come out of the household money. Lately Milt spent some of his to rig up a little observatory on the roof where he can watch the stars.

Besides the MOMOs, we have always run three checking accounts. I have mine and he has his and we have a joint account. Milt takes care of all our household expenses. I take care of my professional expenses, which are high, buy my clothes and pay the taxes for both of us, which are also high. The money in our joint account goes for vacations, trips to Iowa to see Lisa and her family, presents, that sort of thing. I highly recommend the three-account system. Both partners should be able to spend money without accounting for it. Sybil Ferguson agrees. She says that "If a woman works outside the home, she needs to be able to spend money on extras that she might not be able to afford on his budget. Both of them must agree on what these extras are, so they are not pulling separately, but both husband and wife need to have their own money. A woman needs to be able to buy the cosmetics or the dress she wants without having to ask her husband."

Some successful women admit that they fight with their husbands about money, but they insist that their disagreements are not serious, that they do not affect their relationship. "We have problems," says Linda Tarry, "because I believe that what is his is mine—and what is mine is mine. From day one, that has always been a problem, but one that we can and do live with."

This attitude is more prevalent among working wives than among their husbands. Research shows that twice as many working wives as husbands feel that "mine is mine—and yours is too."

"My husband pays the major household bills," Linda says, "and I handle my own personal bills. We usually share when there are lavish expenditures on the children. For a lot of things we just say, 'Who's going to take care of this one?' and he'll say 'I will' or 'You will.' On major items—like a new sofa for the living room—we'll say, 'We need this' and we buy it. We have problems about money, but there's not a great big brouhaha about it in our house."

Chris Boe Voran reports that she was really stupid about the way money was handled in her first marriage. "There were money difficulties," Chris says. "My first husband convinced me that the right thing to do was to put my paycheck into the checking account and invest his. So I paid the rent, the food, the clothes, everything. What this meant was that I never had any savings. All my money was spent on groceries and rent and the rest of it.

"I would bring this up sometimes, and he would say, 'Well, of course some of the investments are yours. We have a joint investing account. Bla-bla-bla.' The fact was that I had no control over it.

"Then when the time came for the divorce, he said, 'The savings are mine. The assets are mine. I can show that it was my checks that went into the savings and investments. They are my property. Not yours.'

"And I said, 'Wait a minute. Then you owe me for rent and food and clothing and cars and everything else for all the years that you put your paycheck into savings and I paid all our expenses.' It was a real problem in the divorce. I think I got screwed. How could I have been so stupid?

"In my present marriage, we have an arrangement that I like. When I was working, we paid according to our means. Just for example, suppose I earned a hundred thousand a year and Bryce earned three hundred thousand. Then I would pay one-third of our living expenses and he would pay two-thirds. We were each on our own for clothes and that sort of thing. If you need a new refrigerator, you each contribute your percentage. But if you want to buy a Nikon instead of a Kodak, that's different. That comes out of your own money that doesn't go for living expenses. So fine, go ahead and buy the Nikon if you've got the money.

"Now that I'm home with our son and not working, I have my own checking account and my own investment account, and so does my husband. Sometimes I feel as if we have accounts up to our ears. My husband, a partner in a law firm, gets paid quarterly. Every quarter, I get a dollar amount that we have agreed on paid into my account. Then we have a joint account that pays for my clothes and my car and his clothes and his car and our vacations. If I want to buy a thousand-dollar suit and I don't want him to know, I can get four hundred dollars from the joint account—that's a reasonable price for a suit—and the other six hundred can come out of my savings."

Some successful women and their husbands subscribe to the theory that what is mine is mine and what is yours is yours. In one study of couples whose median earnings were $90,000, sociologist Rosanna Hertz of Wellesley College found that half preferred to handle their money separately. This proportion did not hold true in my particular sample of successful women, but there were those who kept their funds separate. They tended to be quite relaxed about it.

Sally Quinn and her husband, Ben Bradlee, editor of *The Washington Post*, operate on their own money.

"We keep our money totally separate," Sally says, "and we've never had any disagreements about it. I pay for my own clothes and usually pay for decoration-type things, which is what I enjoy doing. If I redo a room in our house, I'll pay for the chintz and I'll go out and buy antiques, all that kind of thing. Ben pays the sort of larger bills, the maintenance bills. He pays for the things that make things run and I pay for the things that look good.

"We would never have a joint bank account. Ben says he would never know how much money there was. And neither would I. I would be writing checks and he would be writing checks and we would never know where we were."

"Sometimes I'll go out and buy big stuff for our son, Quinn, and sometimes I'll charge those things and then Ben pays the bill. There is no real system. I'll pay for Christmas presents and he'll pay for some. There are no rules. He has more money than I do, so he spends more money than I do. He pays for more things than I do. We don't keep accounts or budgets, but it generally works out.

"Every once in a while, if I find some beautiful kilim that I want and can't afford, I might say, 'How would you like to pick up this one?' And he'll do it. But things like a kilim—well, a rug is a joint thing, something for both of us."

Heloise and her husband are another couple who keep their finances separate. "David has his and I have mine," Heloise says. "We both contribute to the household upkeep. You see, I supported myself and took care of all my bills and everything from the time I was eighteen. When I got married I was just two months short of thirty. And I said, 'David, I've been doing this a long time. I do things a certain way and I feel comfortable this way. My father was in the military and he got paid every month. And I handle money the way he did. You pay all your bills and what is left over goes into your savings and you can spend it.

"David, on the other hand, has been a plumber and a contractor. For him, the money comes in and then it doesn't and then it does and then it doesn't. That would drive me absolutely crazy. I wouldn't know how much I could spend or how much I could save.

"We decided that the less traumatic way for our relationship was not to have any joint finances. And it works out fine. When it comes to something major that one or the other of us wants, I can say or he can say, 'Well, it's money that I've earned.' I have my savings account and if I want to buy a piece of jewelry or something, then I do and there's no jealousy there. It's the same thing if David wants to buy a new shotgun or something for his boat."

Not all successful women take money management in their stride. There are those who argue, sometimes bitterly, over money, who stew over what they perceive as injustices in the financial arrangements of their marriages. Sometimes their problems are simply those of the early years of marriage, when couples usually have all sorts of problems to work out before shaking "me" and "you" down into a compatible and happy marital "we." Other women feel that their high earning power entitles them to the same kind of say in their private lives as their husbands have—and they bitterly resent being relegated to a secondary rather than an equal role.

What do these women do about it? Most of them talk it out and try to resolve it. They look for solutions, for compromises.

"We have difficulty in handling money," says Nancy Evans. "I have read absolutely every book that has ever come out on the subject. It takes time to actually come up with a system that is both equitable and workable.

"I had been paying our household bills and trying to collect what was in effect rent money from my husband to kick into the household stuff. And it just has not worked. I feel as if I am being put upon and he feels as if he is doing his fair share and neither of us feels happy with the way we are handling our money.

"What we have done is bring in an accountant who, we hope, can be a kind of money manager and help us straighten this out. We are going to this accountant almost as if we were going to a shrink to figure out the best way to do this. The last thing either one of us wants to have to do is worry about the money stuff. There must be some way to do it so it doesn't become an issue.

"It is not so much a matter of disparity in our incomes as it is the day-to-day paying of bills. My husband is a lawyer by training, president of a film-distribution company and a writer. He has always been successful. And I have these feelings of I want him to take care of me, I want him to make a lot of money and take care of me, and I have to talk myself out of this.

"There was a period when he was working on a book and his advance for the book was all the money he had during that period. I felt as if he wasn't making enough money and I remember being resentful. I talked to myself about it. I told myself that I was really not being fair. He had made a commitment to this book and if I could just last it out, it would be okay. And it was.

"But we still haven't solved our money problems."

The marriages of a significant number of successful women have dissolved largely because of money problems—or, more correctly, power struggles. These are marriages in which the wife earns more than her husband, a new phenomenon in marriage that I discuss in the following chapter.

SEVENTEEN

WHAT ABOUT marriages where the wife earns more than the husband? I have one of those marriages, and I speak from experience when I say that it is possible to earn more than your husband and still have a good marriage. But at least 75 percent of the marriage's chance for success depends on the husband. Some men just can't swallow the fact that their wife earns more than they do.

If you remember those studies I cited earlier showing that men whose wives work felt less secure and more depressed than men whose wives do not work, it is easy to understand that when a man's wife earns more than he does it represents a double threat to his manhood. She not only works, but she brings home a bigger paycheck.

"I feel like a kept man," a friend of my husband's once told me. Considering that he earned a six-figure annual salary, one might think that he could take his wife's higher earnings in stride, but no. It rankled.

There was a time not too long ago when only a handful

of men earned less than their wives. But this has changed and is still changing. A recent Census Bureau survey showed that on the whole, about 18 percent of American working wives under the age of twenty-five earned more than their husbands, and 19 percent of those between forty-five and fifty-four, 16 percent between thirty-five and forty-four, and 18 percent of the women between forty-five and fifty-four earned more than their husbands. When it comes to successful women, the percentage shoots way up. A survey of "young achievers," a group defined as executive women under forty, showed that *60 percent* of them earned more than their husbands.

What does this mean in their marriages? Increasing instability, for one thing. Husbands are resentful. And they feel insecure. They worry that their wives will eventually abandon them—and their fears are justified.

Studies show that "families are more likely to break up when women earn more compared to men than when the women earn less," says economist Gary S. Becker of the University of Chicago. And Maureen Anderson, dean of students at Case Western Reserve University in Cleveland, who did a study on women CEO's, found that many of the women who had happy marriages at the time of the study had been married before. They blamed the collapse of their earlier marriages on competition. Most of them went on to marry men who were either as successful as they were or were in fields where there was no real comparison for success.

This was the case with Chris Boe Voran. "My first husband was a man who believed very strongly that your worth as a human being was judged in part by the job you had and the amount of money you made.

"I was a teacher when we were first married. When I left teaching and became a lawyer, especially a lawyer with a very large and prestigious Wall Street firm, I became more worthwhile and more powerful in his eyes. Because of the pay structure of New York City law firms, I very quickly caught up to and passed him in earnings. He reached a point where he could not live with that. He put a lot of pressure on me toward the end of the marriage to give up my job. He just could not deal with my success, and he became hostile. The relationship deteriorated very badly when I began earning more money than he did."

The fact is that it is much more difficult to maintain a happy marriage when you earn as much as or more than your husband. It is not just that you earn more, he also resents your absorption in your career. He feels he is competing with your work for the attention he considers his due. And you are struggling to be allowed to devote as much time and energy to your work as he does to his.

Janet Edart (not her real name), who handles political campaigns on the gubernatorial and senatorial levels, found that money and the success that it represented were closely related to the failure of her marriage.

"I think the moment a woman makes a dollar more than her husband, the whole dynamic of the relationship starts to go askew. All the role models are out the window. It takes a very secure man to deal with a woman who makes more. If they start out even or with the man ahead and then the woman pulls up even with him or ahead, it is not comfortable.

"My husband was a very powerful man and made big money. But I came to realize, 'Hey, wait a minute! I earn impressive dollars too.' I realize that what hurt our marriage was that my confidence in my earning ability gave me the confidence to ask for equal time in the marriage.

"What I mean by that was saying, 'No, wait a minute. I'm tired. . . . No, wait a minute. I want to tell you *my* problems tonight. . . . No, I have to work tonight. . . . No, wait a minute. I want to invite *my* guest tonight.'

"I kept saying to him, 'Wait a minute. I'm valuable too. I'm a real earner too. I'm allowed to feel depressed at night too. I'm allowed to want to stay home instead of going out to a party. I'm allowed to feel tired and not want to make love tonight.' It hurt the marriage."

Janet eventually faced a divorce. It was not only money that came between them, it was her struggle for equal power. She wanted to have her work and her needs taken as seriously by her husband as he expected her to take his work and his needs. As she put it, "I married a strong man, but he didn't want equality."

Then there is Kim Salesbury (again not her real name), who worked for the same corporation as her husband. They started out working in different departments, earning roughly the same money. Kim was ambitious and a hard worker. Her husband was easygoing and not at all ambitious. Kim soon pulled ahead, got almost yearly promotions and salary increases.

"My career has been quite successful and his has not," Kim says. "This is difficult because good things are always happening to me and nothing good has happened to him careerwise for quite some time.

"Now, if he were here, he would tell you that this does not affect our marriage. But I say it does. There are subtle ways that I see it affecting our marriage. Lately he has been saying that I wear the pants in the family. Well, that tells me something. He says it in a teasing way, but to me it is a little bit more than teasing.

"I say to him, 'Do you resent my getting this promotion?' And he says, 'No, it's not that at all.'

"But it is."

Kim has since separated from her husband, preparatory to filing for divorce.

Some men are able to take their wife's success in stride. There may be awkward moments, but for the most part they surmount them.

"It was difficult for my husband sometimes," Joan Rivers says. "He was always saying, 'This is Edgar Rosenberg comma Joan Rivers' husband comma,' and that I think was a very difficult pill to swallow for twenty years."

Sybil Ferguson discovered to her dismay that many Diet

Center counselors were having marital problems because they were doing so well. There were a lot of divorces.

"You have to understand that every Diet Center counselor has lost weight the Diet Center way. Some of them have lost as much as a hundred pounds. When they lose that kind of weight, they want to tell the world about it. I am talking about a specific category here, women who have been obese, women who felt they were failures, who had never been achievers in any area. When Diet Centers helped them to lose their weight and led them into a field that they truly understood, they began to be successful as counselors.

"They started making more money than their husbands, and their husbands became very resentful. There were separations and divorces.

"Now I tell all my counselors who suddenly find that they are making more money than their husbands to realize that first of all, their husband feels threatened, because she is now excited about her body and the way she looks. He feels threatened and jealous. Threatened because her money gives her independence, jealous because she is so excited about her job and also because she is more attractive now.

"If she wants to keep her husband happy, she has to make sure he knows that he is the man of her life. She has to build his ego. She needs to make him feel that he is the most important part of her life. I explain that the husband will have an inferiority complex if the wife is not very, very careful. She has to make him feel special so that he has that security.

"For most of our counselors, Diet Center is a family business. And this is good. It keeps the family together. We not only have husbands who quit their jobs to manage product supplies and the ordering and the bookkeeping, we have their children who come in and clean the offices, so they are involved and earn money too.

"It is very difficult if the husband is not involved. In fact, they come to really dislike the business if they are not. We recognize this and try to involve the husbands. We want them to come to our conventions. We want them to catch the excitement of what their wife is doing and the feeling of achievement when she helps other women lose weight and be happier."

This kind of sensitivity to a husband's feelings is the key to sustaining a marriage. It does not always work. Some husbands are so threatened by a wife who earns more or is more famous than they are that nothing a woman can do will keep the marriage together. But given a husband who loves you and is happy for your success and has a fairly strong ego, a woman can smooth over the rough spots and keep her higher earnings or status from being an issue in the marriage.

Lynn Redgrave assured me that there has never been any competition in her marriage. Her husband is an actor, and I have observed over the years that very seldom are a husband and wife who are both actors on the same level when it comes to success and career. "This has not been a factor over the twenty-odd years of our marriage," Lynn told me. "Our careers have not been on an even plane, but it does not matter.

"I'm very fortunate in being married to John in that he was a terribly successful child actor in England. You might describe him as the male Shirley Temple of England, he was that well known. But as so often happens with child actors, particularly the ones who are enormously successful, there is a terrifying moment when you are not this cute person anymore. You are changing into something else.

"John had the good sense to sign up with the merchant navy when he was old enough. He went around the world for four years, and no one knew he had been that famous child actor. Then he emigrated to Canada and became an actor again.

"Since he has experienced huge success and known both the ups and downs, I don't think he has that impassioned drive to be a success now that people who have never experienced success often have. Of course he loves it when something he does goes well and is successful, but he has been a success and he knows the downside. He has helped with my successful times and my down times, because he knows what they are like.

"John enjoys and supports my successes in a totally unselfish way. We feel that everything I do successfully is really a combined effort. I may be the one on the stage, but whatever I am is because of what he brings to our life and in practical terms, of the advice he gives me. I don't think he has the slightest ego problem about what I do. He says that he does not.

"The only times—and they are more annoying than anything—are when we go to a party and are introduced to someone and that person simply looks at me because I am better known and ignores John. This is terribly bad manners. I think it is probably a little hard for him to take, but I am very sensitive to what is happening and so we kind of talk about it."

At one time Milt and I had our own problems in this area. It was when I was becoming well known because of having won *The Sixty-four Thousand Dollar Question* and Milt was simply my husband, the young doctor. Milt was delighted with my success, and we both benefited from the money. We used most of it to set Milt up in his medical practice. We both agreed that it was the best possible investment we could make.

But there were little indignities that ruffled Milt. One that really stuck in his craw happened after I had given a lecture in New Jersey one evening. As we were leaving the hall, a woman stopped me and asked for my autograph. And then another and another until there was a long line of people, all of them wanting me to sign scraps of paper for them. I had my coat over my arm and it was awkward, so I asked Milt to hold it while I signed autographs. He stood there patiently holding my coat for the better part of half an hour. Finally I realized that he was simmering. As we left, he said something about having found his proper niche in life, coat holder for his celebrity wife. Well, that was enough. I'd had

no idea that he would resent it, but it was the last time I ever
ever ever asked him to hold anything while I signed autographs.

Nowadays when I am with him, I finesse the autograph
sessions. When I am alone, an audience can autograph me
to death. I am flattered that they want my autograph. But
when I am with Milt, we just walk by and I say we have to
rush to make our plane, or whatever.

Milt's basic attitude toward my earning more money than
he does is—Wonderful! The pleasures the money brings to
both of us outweigh any negative feelings. More than that, I
have a husband who has no ego problem. He earns a good
living, sufficient for the two of us to live very comfortably.
He is doing exactly what he wants to do and is highly respected by his medical colleagues. My money simply makes
life pleasanter and more exciting for the two of us.

Somehow it seems that the closer you are, the less un-
healthy competition there is in your lives. When I asked my
daughter, Lisa, if she and her husband, both ophthalmologists practicing together, if there was any competitiveness
between them, she shook her head.

"We each have different strengths, so we are compatible,
not competitive. He specializes in pediatric ophthalmology
and I am more interested in treating problems of the retina.

"Sometimes we disagree on treatment. What we do then
is read everything in the medical literature on the particular
problem. This additional input usually clears up any diver-
gency of opinion we have. If it does not, then we consult the
foremost expert on whatever the problem is and go by what
he or she says."

If there is any rule for coping with the problem of making
more money or having more status than one's husband, it
is—Be sensitive to his feelings. Let him know that you recognize and appreciate his strengths. This is the advice Sybil
Ferguson gives her counselors, and I certainly cannot im-
prove upon it. Lynn Redgrave obviously is always alert to

situations where her husband might feel overshadowed and makes sure that he knows how much she loves and respects him. She also makes him feel part of her success. And I call on my psychological know-how as well as on my knowledge of how Milt reacts to certain situations to prevent his ever feeling diminished by my higher earnings or greater public image.

But sometimes—as with Janet Edart and Kim Salesbury— there is nothing a wife can do. She is faced with a choice between her career and her marriage. It is a hard choice.

PART FOUR

CHILDREN

EIGHTEEN

THE OVERWHELMING majority of the successful women we interviewed—slightly more than 80 percent of the presently or previously married women—chose to have children. Five percent of them had adopted their children. Approximately 10 percent had made a conscious choice of career over children. Of the rest, some had never wanted children. Others wanted a child, but not at this point in their lives. Julia Child told us, "I just never had any. It just happened that way. I regret not having children, but I have never felt deprived not being a mother—although I would love to be a grandmother."

How do these successful women manage to combine their careers and families? Amazingly well, despite the stress, the fatigue, the adjustments and the guilt that seem to be part of every working mother's life. All working mothers, wealthy or not, face the same problem: Who is going to take care of my child while I am at work?

Many of the women we interviewed had dependable full-time help—nannies or housekeepers. Some stopped working for a few years to stay home with their child and when they went back to work relied on full- or part-time help. Others were able to work from home. A few relied on day care of one kind or another.

These women are not representative of the average working mother, in that most of them were able to afford help or a day-care center. As Professor Barbara R. Bergmann of the University of Maryland points out in her book *The Economic Emergence of Women*, a baby nurse or housekeeper may cost more than a working mother earns. As for day-care centers, even if a woman can afford the fee, she may not be able to find an opening.

In Connecticut, there are more than 90,000 children under six whose parents work. There are only 55,000 places in day-care centers and homes that care for three to six children. On Long Island, which comprises two counties of New York State, there are more than 20,000 children whose parents work. And there are only 5,000 places available in day-care centers. On the other side of the continent in California, Dr. Karen Hill-Scott, a professor in the graduate school of architecture and urban planning at UCLA, found that in Los Angeles County there are 795,000 children under thirteen whose mothers work outside the home and only 531,000 places in child-care centers or licensed day-care homes.

Not all the women I interviewed were ultraprivileged, however. Many have had hard personal and financial decisions to make because of their children. None of them started out successful. All of them earned their success. And for some it came harder than for others. Take Marilyn Moore, for example.

Marilyn holds an executive position today, but there was a time when she was on welfare. "I was nineteen when I got married, and I had three children very quickly," Marilyn reported. "Right now their ages are fourteen, fifteen and sixteen. My second child arrived just one week less than nine months after my first child. A year and a half later I had my third child. Six months after my third child was born, I was divorced. I was twenty-two years old.

"I had started working at a clerical position just before I got divorced. I wasn't able to keep the job, because I did not have a car and I could not find baby-sitters. I had to quit. And then I had to rely on welfare.

"I got another clerical job, and after three years I decided to go back to school. I started at the University of Wisconsin. I worked twenty hours a week and went to college full time. At that time I had the children in an excellent day-care center. I could drop them off in the morning and I did not worry about them once during the day. I knew they were having a good time and that they were having excellent care. When they started school, I arranged for them to go to a school close to the day-care center instead of our neighborhood school, so they could go to the center before and after school.

"Sometimes I look back and think, 'Oh, dear, how did that all work out?' After I graduated from college, I went to Minneapolis. I was working extremely long hours. I had no support system there at all. It was a real difficult time. The children didn't have any day care. They were on their own. They would go to school, come home from school. I would call and tell them what to prepare for dinner. I was a telephone mom. At that time, they were seven, eight and nine. On their own. When I think back, I really don't know how they did it.

"I felt terribly guilty, but I could see no other choices. The reason I went back to school was that I wanted to be financially able to support myself and my children. I also had this drive to prove myself. I have not figured out yet who I was proving myself to. Myself mostly, I think.

"I wanted to have a better life. I wanted my children to have a better life. I knew that if I worked hard I would do well."

Despite her success and the better life it has brought to her and her children, Marilyn still feels guilty. "I just don't think it was right that the children had to be so much on their own in those years when I was struggling to get off welfare and get an education. I still feel guilty. But looking back," she says thoughtfully, "I don't think I had any choices. Except not to do anything. And if I hadn't, where would we all be today? Still on welfare probably."

It does not seem right that Marilyn should feel guilty, but she does. And so do hundreds of thousands of other working mothers. They are bedeviled by guilt. They worry about what it is going to do to their children if they are not home to take care of them. They worry that their children are being deprived because they do not have full-time mothering. They worry about the quality of care they are able to provide for their children. They worry that their children may feel neglected or insecure or unloved.

What do the child-care experts say about all this?

Well, some say that a working mother can have an adverse effect on her child's development and some say that a working mother can have a positive effect on her child's development. My own opinion is that it depends.

These are not weasel words. They are based on my review of what researchers claim to have discovered over the years about the impact of a working mother on her children, my own experience in a family that boasts three generations of working mothers, and the experiences of the working mothers my researchers and I interviewed for this book.

In the 1930s when my sister and I were growing up, most psychologists believed that a mother who worked outside the home was dooming her children to all sorts of insecurities and problems, even to juvenile delinquency. At that time working mothers were an exotic species. Some psychologists felt that the children of these mothers would consider themselves different from their peers and that this would trigger all kinds of psychological trauma.

Today it is the child of a stay-home mother who is liable to feel different, since about two-thirds of the women in this country with children under sixteen work outside the home. But nobody seems to worry that the children of stay-home mothers might feel different and be at risk in any way, although there are studies that indicate that the children of working mothers may be better off in significant ways.

Be that as it may, my mother worked, and my sister and I never felt that we were being shortchanged in any way. Our lives were not particularly different from those of our friends and classmates. There was always someone there when we got home from school. We did all the things the other children did, from piano lessons to roller skating. We never felt different. Yes, Mother went off to work with Dad every morning. That was the way things were at our house. And when our parents were at home, their lives revolved around us. We had a wonderful childhood. And I think Elaine and I grew up to be satisfactory adults. We have good marriages, great children and absorbing careers. Our lives are busy and full of love.

In the 1950s when Lisa was born, the thinking was that a responsible mother should stay at home with her child for at least the first three years, if the child was to develop normally. I took this very seriously. I gave up my teaching and my research to devote myself to Lisa full time for those three years.

It was wonderful for a few months. I was playing house in our tiny apartment and marveling at my baby. But after a while, I was so bored and so tired that I could barely get through the day. Everything became a tremendous effort. The breakfast dishes would still be in the sink when I started to get supper. I used to feel guilty because I was not enjoying every moment of motherhood.

I had never expected to feel this way. I adored Lisa. She had been a very much wanted baby. But the truth is that babies are not terribly stimulating company for hours on end, and we were so poor that even the occasional baby-sitter to liberate me for a few hours was out of the question. I felt like a prisoner, and the hours of my "sentence" crawled by at a snail's pace.

Once I went back to work, I was busy, busy, busy. I was

running from six in the morning until eleven at night, but that awful fatigue that had overwhelmed me when I was home all day was a thing of the past. I suspect that if I had stayed home with Lisa any longer, it might have had a negative impact on her. I have no way of knowing for sure, but I do know that a mother who is bored to distraction is not an ideal mother.

I consider it significant that Lisa, the third-generation working mother in our family, did not even consider staying home for the first three years of her children's lives. She was back at work within months after each child was born, and my grandchildren seem to be thriving both physically and emotionally, to be none the worse for it.

I do not mean that there were no problems as Lisa was growing up. There were times when she resented my career, times when I was not there for her, and I will discuss those later, but all in all, I believe that my career enriched her life.

Today researchers seem to be straddling the fence when it comes to advising women whether or not they should work after they have children and in their assessments of the effect of working mothers on their children.

A five-year study of 573 children in the first, third and fifth grades showed "positive outcomes" in the children of working mothers. "All significant differences in social and academic criteria favored children of employed mothers," Kent State psychologist John Guidubaldi reported. They did better than the children of stay-home mothers in reading and mathematics, had higher IQ scores and were more independent.

Psychologist Lois Wladis Hoffman of the University of Michigan, who has spent decades studying the effects of maternal employment, has found that working mothers encourage independence in their children "more than mothers who do not work." Independence is a desirable trait in children, Professor Hoffman says, and "especially good for daughters." Stay-home mothers, she has found, "often do more for the child than is necessary and thus delay the child's achieving independence."

And citing a study of eight-year-olds that turned up no differences in intellectual, emotional or social development between children with stay-home mothers and children who had been cared for by others, psychologist Sandra Scarr of the University of Virginia told the American Psychological Association that "Parents don't have to be there every minute. Kids who are nurtured lovingly by people other than their parents grow up perfectly normally. We are not cheating our kids by leaving them with loving care-givers," she said, "and we may be doing them some good."

On the other hand, psychologist Edward Zigler, director of Yale University's Bush Center in Child Development and Social Policy, says, "It is scaring everyone that a whole generation of children is being raised in a way that has never happened before."

And psychologist Jay Belsky, professor of human development at Pennsylvania State University, who coauthored a report in 1978 indicating that babies seemed to thrive in day-care centers, changed his mind in 1986, when he wrote that "There is cause for concern and reason to question the prevailing notion that infant care is fine and dandy." He now feared that when a baby spent more than twenty hours a week with a caretaker other than the mother, the baby might not form a strong enough attachment to the mother. He reported that there was evidence that this "insecure attachment" could lead to antisocial behavior when the child started school.

No wonder mothers are confused. Which expert should they believe?

There does seem to be a well-documented risk of more infections among children in day-care centers than in those cared for in their own homes. The American Academy of Pediatrics put out a report prepared by Drs. Ron Haskins and Jonathan Kotch of the University of North Carolina stating that there was definitely more risk of infectious disease for both the children in day care and their families. Most of the illnesses are mild—on the order of sniffles and upset tummies—but there is also a documented danger of more serious problems, such as ear infections and hepatitis and bacterial meningitis.

Until further studies can be carried out, the Academy says that the long-term effects of these day-care illnesses cannot be assessed. Some doctors believe that there is a certain advantage when children come down with some infections when they are young, since the symptoms tend to be less severe than they are later on.

Will your baby grow up to be a juvenile delinquent or emotionally maimed because you pursued a career? Or will your career have a positive influence and help your child grow up to be well balanced, responsible and independent?

No wonder working mothers feel guilty. If anything is wrong with their child, it is all their fault. It certainly is if you believe everything you read in the journals of clinical psychology. Two researchers who reviewed journals of child psychology over a twelve-year span discovered that mothers were blamed for their children's problems five times as often as fathers were. There is, of course, a reason for this. Mothers are the ones who take most of the responsibility for children. Even now, the majority of fathers, even fathers in dual-career families, take far less responsibility for their children than mothers do. As Jane Pauley, cohost of the *Today* show and mother of three, told an interviewer, "Those profiles of the 'new father' are garbage. Garry is a very involved father, but the responsibility is mine."

What I want to tell working mothers right here and now is that—

If you love your child and let her or him know it . . .

If you truly love your work and share your excitement about what you are doing with your child, or if you work because you must to keep the family afloat economically and you share this fact of life with your child . . .

If you familiarize your child with your work and your working place . . .

If you are honest with your child . . .

If you have provided the best care for your child that you can find and afford . . .

If all this is true, then my feeling is that your child will not suffer because you work outside the home and you have no reason to feel guilty.

Dr. T. Berry Brazelton, associate professor of pediatrics at Harvard Medical School and head of the Child Development Unit at Children's Hospital in Boston, agrees. "The fact is," he says, "that over half of the women in this country have to work, either for financial reasons or for psychological ones. . . . If anything goes wrong, the working mother always blames it on the fact that she is working." Things can go just as wrong for the stay-home mother, he observes.

Dr. Brazelton also feels that a working mother need not fear that her baby will not have a strong enough attachment to her as long as the mother has been able to stay home with the baby for the first four months. He considers these months critical in an infant's development, but says that by the beginning of the fifth month, most babies are secure enough to accept a daily separation from the mother.

Some career women feel guilt that stems from a romantic ideal of motherhood, a feeling that a perfect relationship between mother and child is possible.

There are no perfect relationships. This is not a perfect world. Dr. Bruno Bettelheim, the psychologist who has devoted almost half a century to an effort to discover and test what is involved in and required for successful child rearing, says that "People should forget the idea that they are going to be perfect parents and are going to have the perfect child.

There are no perfect children. There are no perfect parents."
Working mothers, he says, should spend less time feeling
guilty.

The group of successful women whom I and my researchers interviewed probably feel less guilt than most working
mothers. They are all intensely practical and sensible women
who have made choices and accepted the trade-offs.
These women know they are doing the best they can. None
of them consider themselves perfect parents, although a few
might believe they have perfect children. Few of them consider their child-care arrangements perfect either, but they
are the best they can devise. In the following chapter fourteen
of these women tell how they manage.

NINETEEN

CAREER WOMEN are often thought to be a separate breed—competent, brittle, cool, even cold. Nothing could be further from the truth in the cases of the working mothers we interviewed. They are passionate about their work, true enough, but in most instances, their lives revolve around their families, around their children.

These women had children because they really wanted them. They understood that children would complicate their already complicated lives, but this was a trade-off they accepted happily. A surprising number of them chose to put their careers on hold and stay home with their children for the first few years, even though some of them discovered, just as I had three decades earlier, that life at home with a child left something to be desired. While motherhood was challenging and absorbing, they missed the stimulation and excitement they had found in their work. Even so, they did not return to work until they were sure that their child was ready to face life without Mother for eight hours a day.

Chris Boe Voran, who gave up her prestigious job in a Wall Street law firm when she was within months of being made a partner because she felt her hectic life prevented her from becoming pregnant, found that life with Baby was not all strawberries and cream.

"I enjoy being with my son," she said, "although there are times when I am with him that I'm saying, 'Oh, God! I'm so bored! I'm so BORED!' I guess it is a cynical thing to say, but sometimes I stay and play with him because if I don't, he screams. And if he is screaming, I can't sit down and read or go do something in another room. It really gives me a stomach ache.

"What I am dealing with now is, How does a mother arrange her life to get things for herself while she is also keeping things going for the baby? It is a terrible adjustment learning to deal with these little people and their schedules, even when you have help. I have help four days a week for him and he still takes an enormous amount of my time. I am tired and bored a lot, which is a mother condition."

"I didn't really enjoy it," says Joyce Buchman, who stayed home until her younger child was six. "I would much rather have been facing the gun in a boardroom with forty people than sitting on a park bench watching my kids climb on the monkey bars.

"In retrospect, though, I'm glad I did it. I gained a lot. First of all, I would have felt guilty if I had not stayed home. And second, I'm not so sure the children would have turned out so great if I hadn't been with them during those years. I am very close to my kids, and I think a lot of it is that I was there all those years."

Felice Schwartz is inclined to believe that her children would have been better off if she had been home less. "When my first child was born, I had someone who came in during the day to care for her when I was working. When I was pregnant with my second, I decided to take some time off. If I could do it over again, I would not take off full time, as

I did. I would have taken off part time, because I am much too goal-oriented and energetic. It would have been better for me and for my kids if I had just cut back to working half time.

"I think it was guilt that pushed me to it. The guilt was a function of that time, of society's pressures. I think all of us in my generation felt it. If I had spent more of my life at home with my kids, I don't think it would have been a good time."

There were other women who did not find their time at home so oppressive. They managed to keep one foot in the working world, which may have made the difference for them.

"I took almost three years off when Juliet was born, but all that means is that I was not working at a full-time, salaried job," Gillian Sorensen said. "I was very active in political work and also did some volunteer work.

"The housekeeper I have now I found when Juliet was six weeks old, and she has been with us ever since—thirteen years. It has been very important to have someone who loves Juliet and knows the family and whom I can trust."

Lynn Gilbert said, "I stayed home for three and a half years and worked part time in my husband's office during those years. My son was three and a half and my daughter was a year old when I went back to work.

"I began by working three days a week and then built it up to four days. I worked four days a week for maybe eight or nine years. I would be home one day a week when I would do my car pooling, marketing, dentist and doctor appointments. I would do all the motherly things that day. I had a housekeeper who stayed with the children on the four days I worked."

And then there were women like Lana Jane Lewis-Brent who went right back to work, who never considered staying home. "I took about a week off when my son was born and was back in the office full time at the end of ten days," she says.

"My husband and I had planned to find someone to live in. It took quite a bit of time and several housekeepers before we located someone who has enjoyed living in our home and taking care not only of our son, but of our needs as well. My mother lives near us, and he visits her a couple of times a week for a few hours, and about once a month he will spend the night with her."

Jacqueline Leo also went back to work almost immediately, but not by choice. "I had a C-section," she said, "but I was back at work four weeks later because of a disgraceful company policy at the magazine where I was working at that time. This was a company that in every other way was terribly benevolent, but they had a medieval approach to pregnancy.

"It was hard to get back into a business mode and carry on, but no, I don't regret not being home. You make a choice. You can't go into the whole prospect of parenting at this stage of one's life without having sort of figured it out. It is silly, in a way, to think of a great loss if you are not home between birth and age two and not think of a great loss when they are fourteen . . .

"Alexandra is three now. We do what we can of a morning. We are early risers. We try to find a half-hour to cuddle and snuggle and get in bed with each other and just be delicious with one another. It is a very lovely way to start anyone's day. And then when we get home in the evening we try to have a meal together. My mother helps out, but the baby-sitter has the brunt of getting her bathed and ready for bed and all that. But we have our time together, and it's good time and we do share."

Karen Nussbaum depends on a child-care center. "I like a day-care center as opposed to having someone in the house," she says. "I like the idea that they are in a situation where

there are supervisors, where the people are all accountable
and you know what is going on, where they have a program.
You know they are not just sitting watching television.

"There are problems in a day-care center. You are never
completely satisfied. I certainly have guilt at various times
about whether this is good enough for the boys. We have
just moved them to a center that is closer to where we live.
My younger son is having a hard time adjusting. This is his
second day there. He is crying, and I feel awful about it.
What can I say? I feel like I'm ruining his life. But I know
I'm not. I know that by next week he'll be fine. I took vacation
days so I could be with him for these two days. It is just a
very hard adjustment for him to make. And it's incredibly
painful for me as well as for him while it's happening.

"My older son loves the new place. He's really excited about
it. He didn't want to leave today. It is just that my younger
boy is at a stage where it is hard for him to make that kind
of change.

"My husband and I both travel a lot on business. We have
worked out a pretty satisfactory method of checking with
each other before we schedule any dates. When I am away,
he takes care of the kids, and when I'm there, I'm responsible
for them.

"We've had a couple of near disasters. People in my office
joke about our needing a locker at the airport where we could
stash the kids while one of us is taking off and the other is
just landing, but it has worked out pretty well all in all. The
fact that they are never without one of us means that one of
us can be away on business and it is not a disruption for the
children. It is not like there is some third person taking care
of them. They are always with a parent."

Lynn Redgrave, who was named one of the eight "Out-
standing Mothers of 1987" by the National Mother's Day
Committee, changed her arrangement for child care when
she had her third child. It was a matter of learning from
experience.

"We have two children who are very close together in age. Eighteen and sixteen now. When they were little, we had a live-in, full-time nanny who could drive, could cook a bit, could do all sorts of things. If we were all going on the road together, she would come too. She was very capable and, if necessary, could get on a plane a week later and bring the children with her, or whatever. When they got older, both of them boarded for a while at a school where they could come home most weekends. The school was about an hour and a half's drive from where we lived.

"Annabelle, our youngest, is five now, and we have done things a bit differently with her. First of all, we took her everywhere with us the first two years. We never left her at home. We never even left her for a night for the first two years. Now we have someone who lives with us Monday through Friday.

"We realized that there were pros and cons of having someone who took as much responsibility as the first nanny did. When you give someone that much responsibility, you must also give up something. When the nanny says, 'Look, the burden is on me right now, therefore it must be done my way,' you give in, either because it is the right thing to do or sometimes because it is the path of least resistance. Since you desperately need that person's help, you don't want to ruffle her feathers.

"My older daughter and I have talked about this. In retrospect, I think I sometimes backed off in certain situations, and my daughter did not feel free to talk about things that were troubling her for fear of rocking the boat. I never want that to happen again. That is why we are much more in charge of absolutely everything that Annabelle does.

"Of course, we have the added advantage now of her having an older brother and sister. Between the wonderful lady who lives with us during the week and our own teen-agers and their friends, we have a big support group. All of them are a loving extended family for Annabelle. I think she has it pretty good. And we do too. We get to enjoy her and share huge chunks of her day.

"John and I share the responsibility fairly equally. Not always equally at the same time, because sometimes what I am doing means that he has got the burden. Then there are times when I do more. I did a play in New York for about four months, and the way we split it up was that Annabelle spent the first month in California with him, the next month she was with me in New York and then back to John for a month and the last month with me again."

Most of the women we interviewed were determined, like Lynn Redgrave, to be as much a part of their children's lives as possible. Mary Cunningham wants to be sure that she is completely involved in her children's lives. "When Mary Alana was born, I did not want a live-in nanny," she said.

"My mother worked. She was a single mother and supported four children. I don't know how she did it, but she did, and she was a very loving mother. I think that because of the role model I had in my mother, I have somehow set that as my challenge. If she could do it, I can do it. That is what a role model is all about. It makes you believe you can do things that other people tell you are impossible.

"So I did not go for the live-in nanny. Nor did I want to leave Mary Alana off somewhere unless I absolutely had to. I am fortunate in that Bill and I earn enough so that that kind of option is not one I have to take. I wanted to find something that would be comfortable in terms of the economics and the emotional constraints of the situation.

"For me what was comfortable turned out to be a family friend, Mary Kenney, who had been a pediatric nurse for thirty-two years and had had enough. I had to have a cesarean, and she helped me when I came home with Mary Alana. We became so close that at the end of a couple of weeks, I said, 'I would love to have you stay here anytime you are available. I don't even know if I should ask you.'

"And she said, 'I'm so glad you did. It is exactly what I want to do at this time in my life.'

"I go to the office four out of seven days a week usually, and she comes on those days. When I have to work late, she takes it in her stride. She and her husband live in the next town, and he is used to her working long days and uneven schedules. So what I have is not an everyday kind of thing, but she is literally a telephone call away. And she is a very flexible, very competent, very loving person. It is like having a friend come over when you need some help."

We interviewed Mary again after her second child, a son, was born. He arrived eleven days early by cesarean section.

"It is wonderful to have a grand plan, a strategy," she said, "but you must always build flexibility into any strategy, because you cannot predict precisely what is going to happen in every situation. In this case, Mary Kenney, who was going to stay with Mary Alana while I was in the hospital, called me the night before I went in. Her husband was seriously ill and had to undergo three weeks of medical treatment immediately. He needed her at home.

"My mother, who is almost seventy, came to the rescue. She stayed with Mary Alana while I was in the hospital and stayed on to help me afterwards until Mary Kenney came back. Mom and Mary Alana became very close, and it gave me a chance to bond comfortably with little William. It also helped me feel less torn about not doing my job with Mary Alana, who was going through all the reactions typical of a year-and-nine-months-old child.

"Mary Kenney came back after the three weeks, and what I did was cut back on her hours. That has meant that I have to be a lot more flexible in terms of my work. I do more from home. I keep the office things flowing by correspondence and telephone. I dictate fifteen to twenty letters a day over the telephone. And I have cut out client contact for the time being.

"If you are not accustomed to planning, I think two children and a job could drive you crazy. But my whole life has been geared to planning, so I kind of strategically planned our lifestyle around these two little children. And it has worked, up to a point. You have to be flexible. The greatest need gets the greatest care."

Carole Sinclair is divorced and has one child. When Wendy was born seven years ago, Carole was chairman of the Marketing Committee at Doubleday and the first woman to be appointed to Doubleday's publishing board. She did not expect to have another child and was resolved that Wendy would not be relegated to the care of a nanny or a housekeeper for more than a few hours a day. In spite of her high-pressure job and long working hours, she manages to be with her daughter most of the child's waking hours.

"I worked up until the day she was born and took a month off afterwards. My secretary came over every day with my mail and that sort of thing. Once I was back at work, instead of having business lunches in restaurants, I had them catered in my apartment. This meant I could see my baby in the middle of the day. That first year I came to work late and went home early, but I did a lot of work at home. The baby nurse—I had a live-in baby nurse—told me that I was there every moment Wendy was awake.

"Since she was born, I have only made one business trip without her—three days, and I couldn't sleep the whole time. Ever since, she has gone with me.

"I am up before six and with Wendy until eight thirty, when I drop her off at school. I usually have lunch with her once a week. Every night, no matter what I'm doing, I leave my office at five thirty and go home and have dinner with her, even if I have to do something else later. I'm with her after dinner until at least eight o'clock. I admit it affects my social life, but she is only going to be a little girl once.

"A couple of weeks ago when I took Wendy to school, another mother came up to me. She does not work and she arrives in a chauffeured car every morning to drop her little girl off. She said, 'I see you here every day and I just found out you have a job. Is it full time?' I told her it was, and she said, 'Well, isn't that wonderful!' and whisked away.

"I have observed on the occasions when I can get to Wendy's class functions that half the people in the room are babysitters or baby nurses, even for the kids whose mothers don't work.

"I would absolutely bet my savings that I spend more hours during the week with Wendy than most nonworking mothers spend with their kids. Many of Wendy's friends never have dinner with their parents, but I have always believed that this is a pivotal time of day and a child should never have to be alone then. No matter how good your housekeeper is, she isn't the mother.

"On spring vacation I took Wendy and one of her friends to Washington and showed them everything from the White House to the zoo. When we got back, the other child's mother said that she would never have done it in a million years and how could I stand it? And I said that I loved it and that I thought the kids did too and I liked building memories for the children.

"The other day Wendy told me that lots of her friends wish I were their mommy. I can't tell you how great that made me feel."

Some successful women found themselves staying home indefinitely after their children were born. Some, like Julie Nixon Eisenhower, had always planned to do this; others, like Linda Grant, had expected to keep on working, but found that their baby exerted a stronger pull on them than they had ever expected. "I would be sitting at the office writing a story and I would look at his picture and start to daydream and wonder what he was doing and then suddenly whatever story I was doing for the paper didn't seem very important. And I felt I wasn't seeing enough of him," Linda said.

No matter how it came about, these women seemed to enjoy every moment. The boredom that used to drive me up the wall when I stayed home did not exist for them at all.

. . .

For writers like Julie Nixon Eisenhower and Sally Quinn, staying home with the children did not seem to represent much of a trade-off. They thought they could always find a few hours a day to write. But it did not work out that way.

"I was working on my book about my mother," Julie said, "and I actually stopped work for almost three years after Alex was born because I was so involved with the children. What I have done since is basically work part time.

"I am intensely interested in the children and their development. I find it very exciting watching that development. Also, I just don't feel that people that you hire can give your children the attention that you would give them, the patience that a mother can summon up even though she feels totally out of patience. It is different when it is your child.

"I find it hard to delegate the responsibility of the children to other people. I want to be the one getting them off to school and the one greeting them when they get home. It was very difficult for Tricia and me that our parents had to be gone so much during the political campaigns when we were so young. It was hard to be left behind, and sometimes my mother was not able to get the right child care. I think Tricia and I survived because my parents—and I don't know how they did this, but when they were home, they were really home. Their home was totally child-centered."

Sally Quinn decided to have a child after she took a leave from her reporting job to write a novel. "When you are writing a novel, you really don't write more than three or four hours a day. Our lives were settling down to a whole different rhythm and pace. There really was room for a child.

"After Quinn was born, he was extremely sick," Sally said. "He had open-heart surgery when he was three months old. He was in the hospital a lot. Ben and I were in the emergency room all the time. We were both wiped out, professionally and emotionally. And Ben had to run a newspaper.

"It became clear that someone had to be on top of Quinn's

situation medically all the time, and that had to be me. I was
at home and I was the mother.

"I would write when I could. It wasn't like he was deathly
sick every single day. There would be two or three weeks at
a time when he was doing quite well. I always found blocks
of time, two or three hours here and there, that I could write.
But then there were times when he would get over a bout of
being sick and I would try to write and I was drained. I would
go sit in my office and nothing would happen. I went through
a period of about six months where I didn't write a word.
That was hard.

"But there was never any question of somebody else taking
care of him. I had waited for forty-one years to have a baby,
and I didn't have him so I could turn him over to somebody
else. I wanted to spend time with him. I knew that at some
point in a few years he would be in school full time and then
I would never see him as much.

"I didn't think that taking three or four years out of my
life to be with my baby was a great sacrifice. It was what I
wanted to do. He is a fabulous child. I love him more than
I could ever have imagined loving anybody in my life."

Linda Grant was forty-three when her son was born. She
had not planned to stop working—but as it turned out, she
said, "I stopped working on his first birthday.

"The *Los Angeles Times* had offered me a promotion that
required moving to Los Angeles from New York. I asked for
a number of concessions—if I could work three out of four
weeks a month or if I could take three months off in the
summer. I looked into whether they were going to have on-
site day care. They were not prepared to offer me any concessions. And I am not really prepared to criticize them for that.
In many ways their arguments were sound. Anyway, that was
that.

"That first year when I was still working, it was very rough.
I felt I was not seeing enough of the baby and that things
were not being done well.

"My husband tried his best to pitch in. There were times when we would have to call on neighbors and friends for help. If I had kept on working, we would have had to get a live-in person. As the baby got older, I became very interested in his development. I really wanted to spend more time with him than I was able to when I was working.

"What I have discovered is that staying home with my child has been almost all pleasure. I think there is more than one way to raise children. For some women it is impossible to stay home, and I don't think they should be criticized. But for me, it would have been really all wrong to keep on working."

One way or another, these women have arranged for their children to be cared for while they are working. Only a few admit to feeling guilty—and usually only now and then. As I said earlier, these are intensely practical women. They do the best they can and do not waste time and energy in self-reproach just because their best may fall somewhat short of perfection.

TWENTY

THE BIG crunch for most working mothers comes when a child is sick. It is a time when many women have to make hard, often agonizing decisions. An ailing child is the Achilles' heel of even the most careful child-care arrangements. A youngster who is running a fever or has diarrhea or is throwing up cannot be left at the day-care center. Making emergency arrangements is seldom easy or satisfactory. Marilyn Moore, who carried the double load of working at a job and studying for her college degree, said, "If they were a little bit sick, my mother would take them. If they were sick enough where they were going to throw up, she did not want them and I would stay home." She had no choice but to forfeit a day's pay and miss a day's classes.

Karen Nussbaum, whose children are also in day care, copes by sharing the responsibility with her husband. "It depends on which parent is more free," she said. "Sometimes I stay home. Sometimes my husband does. There is an element of keeping score—who did what last and therefore the other has to do it this time."

Even if you have a full-time person at home, the sick child wants Mommy. "I have a nanny," Pat Collins says, "but even if she is there, if the children are sick, they want Mother. Andrew came down with impetigo the other day. Our nanny was there, but he didn't want her with him—only Mom. I was the one he wanted to read the stories and play the games and listen to the records with him. I think it is normal. I think if he didn't want Mom, something would be very wrong."

But what if Mother can't be there to read the stories and so on? Sometimes Mother just can't make it. She has career obligations that have priority. This is one of the trade-offs—if you work, you cannot always stay home when your child is ill.

What happens then?

"You have a crisis of conscience," says Lynn Redgrave, "as you drive off to the theater or the movie set and your child is lying at home with a fever. This is always the hardest part of it for a working mother.

Lynn, who grew up in the tradition of "the show must go on" no matter what, said, "If I have a show to do, I would not stay away because my child was sick. There are jobs when one can take time out, but acting is a job where it is unacceptable. You can't say to an audience that has bought tickets for that evening, 'Sorry, I won't be there.' At least, I don't think you should."

Barbara Hendricks, whose concert and opera dates are made months, sometimes years, beforehand, is in the same position. "It is hard," she says. "Not too long ago I was in New York singing at the Metropolitan and the children were home in Switzerland with my husband. He took our son skiing and the child broke his leg. When I heard that, I wanted to go home. But I had two performances to do plus a Saturday broadcast for the Metropolitan. I really had to think about it.

"I talked to my sister who has two children and she asked, 'Is he still in the hospital?' He wasn't, so she said, 'If he's home, I don't think that it is so bad you have to jump on a plane tonight and go back.'

"You have to weigh the situation. If I had felt that my son really needed me, there would have been no conflict. My family comes first. But I try to be unsentimental about it. In this case, his father was there with him. And I had an obligation. While this particular performance at the Metropolitan did not hinge on me, often the public has bought tickets just because I am singing. The Metropolitan would not have been happy about my leaving.

"I called him the next day and he was in good spirits. I think I missed being with him more than he missed being with me."

But these were the exceptions. The majority of these very successful women stayed home when a child was ill, even when they had excellent help at home. I got the impression these women would move mountains in order to be with their child. Perhaps not literally mountains, but they would do whatever had to be done. Even lie.

"It was hard for me to stay home when I had to report to a network," Pat Collins said. "It took a little doing. I can't remember ever asking for time off because my child was sick when I was at ABC or CBS. The last thing I wanted to do was make it tough for the next woman coming along. I didn't want to give some male chauvinist the excuse that he won't hire a woman because 'The last one here! God! Every time I turned around she had a sick kid.'

"I would never admit to having a sick child. You have to come up with a fib. I would say something like 'Well, I have to leave now because I have to go read Clint Eastwood's dental charts' or some such thing. Fortunately, now that I have my own company I have a little more control over my schedule."

Significantly, few of these women expected—or wanted—their husbands to take time off when a child was home sick. They wanted to be there themselves.

"I always stayed with Melissa when she was ill," Joan Rivers told me. "It was my responsibility. I never wanted to give it up. I didn't want to let Edgar do half of it. I wanted to be the mother, and I made sure that I got all the perks. Staying with Melissa when she was ill was part of the perks."

And Linda Tarry says, "I would stay home, but it has nothing to do with it being my responsibility. I was raised in a family, in a culture, where the mother can have that—how can I say it?—that sixth sense. If the fever is soaring, Mother will know before Father, due to some innate something God has given her. I really believe that."

Linda is not too far from the truth. There *is* an "innate something." Scientists have discovered that the need to nurture and care for her children is one of the deepest needs a woman has. It belongs to the group of needs called Prepotent Needs.

Animal research has shown that mothering or nurturing is the second-strongest of these very primitive needs. The landmark study that established these needs has been duplicated over and over by generations of psychology students.

The basic mechanism of the experiment measuring Prepotent Needs consists of two metal boxes that are separated by an electrified grid. In a series of trials, rats that have been deprived of something are placed in the first box and the item of which they have been deprived is put in the second box, which is called the Goal Box.

A hungry rat is placed in the first box. There is food in the Goal Box.

A rat that has just given birth is placed in the first box. Her pups are in the Goal Box.

A thirsty rat is placed in the first box. Water is in the Goal Box.

A rat is placed in the first box and the air is removed from that box. The Goal Box has air.

In each instance, the door of the first box is opened and the number and intensity of electric shocks that the rat will endure in its mad scramble across the electrified grid to get to the Goal Box is carefully measured.

Rats repeatedly sustained the strongest shocks for the greatest number of times to get to the Goal Box with air. The rats sustained almost as many shocks to get to their pups in the Goal Box. Water was the third-strongest need. And then came food.

An interesting footnote: male rats do not experience the same need to nurture their young. It has been established, however, that the nurturing need can be created in male rats by injecting them with female hormones.

Not every finding based on animal research is equally valid for humans, but the Prepotent Needs seem to be universal. The innate need of a mother to nurture her child, particularly when the child is small, is extremely strong. Mothers who put everything aside in order to stay at home with an ailing child are simply obeying this primitive need. And mothers whose career obligations prevent them from staying home suffer those guilt-ridden crises of conscience Lynn Redgrave mentioned.

TWENTY-ONE

Now, JUST a postscript about guilt. It is a rare mother—working or stay-home—who escapes guilt. Even if you believe you are doing the best you can and your child is thriving, there are times when you will be made to feel guilty. And you know who the guilt-maker is? Your beloved child. Children seem to be born knowing how to play Mother like a violin. And the tune is always the same: How could you have done this to me? What kind of mother are you?

Once a mother understands what is behind this guilt-making, she can try to guiltproof herself a bit. It is perfectly normal behavior. When Baby is born, the whole world is centered on him. The infant does not know where he stops and the rest of the world starts. When you see a baby sucking his fingers or toes, this is early learning. Baby is discovering his physical limits.

We are self-centered from the word go. Back in the sixteenth century, the astronomer Copernicus had a terrible time trying to convince contemporary scientists that the sun did not revolve around the earth, but quite the contrary: the earth revolved around the sun.

In the same way, children tend to believe that their small worlds revolve around them. And when there is evidence to the contrary—when a mother who is told at the dinner table that she is supposed to bake cookies for the swimming-team bake sale the next day says that it is impossible because she has a report to write that night—the child is offended and startled. What is going on here? Am I not the center of my mother's universe? And Mother, like as not, will be found in the kitchen at two o'clock in the morning baking cookies, the guilt being too much for her to bear.

Mother would do better to stick to her guns and go to bed after she finishes her report. Children have to learn that the world does *not* revolve around them. They also have to learn that mothers need more than a couple of hours' notice if they are to bake cookies or make a costume for the cheer-leader tryouts or whatever. But mothers, being mothers, will either stay up half the night baking or sewing—or lie awake half the night feeling guilty.

One of the laws I lived by when Lisa was young was that I would never make her a promise that I could not keep. When I was not sure that I could show up for the special school assembly or the Thanksgiving pageant, I would say, "I'll do my very best. I'll try hard." And I would try. But when I told her, "I promise I'll be there," she could count on it. The rest of the time she knew that I would do my best, but that there might be circumstances beyond my control.

When I did say, "I promise," nothing short of two broken legs would have stopped me from keeping that promise. And I never, thank God, had to break any promise I made to Lisa. There were inevitably times when I could not get to a field day or a horse show that I had said I would *try* to attend. Lisa would more or less accept my explanations of why I could not make it, but she had a way of making me feel terrible. I practically sweated guilt. And here I was, a psychologist, doing my best to help my daughter understand that there were always going to be times when my absence was unavoidable.

This guilt-inducing exists in all children, whether their mother works outside the home or not; but working mothers, who already have a full load of guilt about what their work may be doing to their children, seem to take it more to heart. Barbara Walters told me that there were many times when career obligations prevented her from attending school events and that her daughter, Jackie, resented it. Once Jackie told her, "Your dream interfered with my dream," and this flooded Barbara with guilt.

"It still brings tears to my eyes when I think of it," she said.

Joyce Buchman is another mother who has been manipulated into guilt. "When Jennifer was in the fifth grade," she said, "she was in a play. She told me I just had to go to this play. I had a really big day coming up and I didn't know how I could do it. But my husband couldn't go, and he said, 'You have to go.' And I said, 'I can't. I have this terribly important meeting. People are flying in from London.'

"Well, I thought about it all night. I couldn't sleep. I decided I would have to go to the play. So I go to the play—and there is only one other woman there. I had canceled my whole day for this. I turned to my daughter and said, 'Jennifer, why am I here?'

"And she said, 'You're here because you're working and working mothers have guilt. The other mothers aren't here because they don't feel guilty.' She was right. That other woman was a working mother too."

And Gillian Sorensen reported, "If there has been any drawback to my working, it is that there have been evenings when Juliet has said, 'Are you going out *again?*' That always makes me feel bad."

It may not make mothers feel better to know that this guilt-inducing behavior stems from the child's firm belief that he or she is the center of the world. But perhaps a mother will feel less guilty if she tells herself that part of growing up is learning that the world is not there for our convenience. And part of her job as a mother is helping her child learn this.

TWENTY-TWO

In a way, the women in this book represent a new generation of pioneers. They are responsible, thoughtful, intelligent, energetic women who see no reason why their lives should be limited by sex or custom. They are women who are seen as "having it all," although they would deny it. They have stripped their lives down to what is meaningful to them.

These women are not typical working mothers. Far from it. They are extremely successful individuals. Their earnings put most of them in the top 5 percent in the country. Those who earn less are in positions where they exert a strong influence on labor, government, industry, women's rights and child care. These women—many of whom are married to prosperous, even wealthy men—work because they want to. Even the women who take a few years off to raise their children always seem to be marking time, consciously or unconsciously, until they can get back to work.

They are good mothers, caring mothers, loving mothers. They sacrifice for their children—sacrifice time for themselves, time for their husbands, friends, leisure—without complaint. The rewards more than compensate for any trade-offs. Some women were amazed at the intensity of the love they felt for their child. They had never expected to experience such intense love for anyone.

They report that their children have enriched their lives: not only their personal lives, but their working lives. "Before I had my son," Karol Emmerich said, "I was almost too intense at work. Since becoming a mother, I have become much more human, and that has made me a better manager."

What these women, with their diverse ethnic and social and economic backgrounds and their varied careers, have in common is a determination to be involved in their children's lives (Chapter Nineteen), and to have their children involved in their own lives both at work and at home.

My parents did the same. I remember how adult it used to make me feel when my father included me in the dinner-table conversation, which he did every night, whether the subject was politics or our summer-vacation plans. He was always an attentive listener to my young opinions.

Milt and I followed the same course with Lisa. She was always very much a part of our lives. She ate dinner with us from the time she was old enough to sit up in her high chair. We always took her on vacation with us. We even took her on our second honeymoon.

I remember once when she was about eight or nine, I took her with me on a weeklong, cross-country speaking tour. I had asked that she be excused from school for that week, pointing out that the trip would be an educational experience.

On the plane returning home, I asked her, "Well, what did you learn from this trip?"

Lisa thought a minute and then, quite seriously, she said, "I learned that you don't take your shoes off when you are at the head table because people can see your feet."

I suppose that was some kind of lesson. But she also learned what I did when I was away from home and what it meant when I said, "I am going to give a lecture at the university" or "I am going to be the after-dinner speaker at the convention." She learned what went on in radio stations and television studios. She learned what a really vast country this is. And probably a host of other things.

Most of the women I interviewed had also made a point of familiarizing their children with their work.

"Two or three times a year during school vacations, I bring Juliet to the office with me so she knows where I am, who I work with, what it is like," Gillian Sorensen said. "It has never been some mysterious place out there."

And Lana Jane Lewis-Brent says, "I incorporate my son into what I do whenever I can. When we have a store opening or a ribbon-cutting ceremony, I make him part of it. When I go to food conventions, I often take him. He gets interested in the new products. Convenience stores have many products that appeal to children. So in a way, he becomes part of me when we are at a convention and he can watch me make buying decisions and 'help' me select products.

"The other day someone asked him, 'What does your mother do?' And he said, 'Don't you know? She's a businesswoman!' I was so proud."

"Whenever it is possible," Lynn Redgrave told me, "I make sure our little one, Annabelle, visits wherever it is I am working. If it is out of town, like for a New York play, she comes to visit for a time. If it is in town and it is more than a few days' work, I make sure she sees where I work, so she knows where I am and the people I am working with."

Carole Sinclair said, "Wendy comes to my office a lot and loves it. When she was five, I asked her what she wanted for her birthday and she said, 'I want an office.'

"I asked her what she meant, and she said, 'I want a desk with your picture on it because you have my picture on your desk. I want a phone and I want an in-and-out box.' So I got her a desk and a phone (nonworking) and an in-and-out box and a picture of me, and she was delighted.

"Last week I had her entire class come to the office. Some of the staff spoke to them and told them how a magazine is made. The kids had a good time and Wendy was thrilled."

"Alexandra loves coming to my office, really really loves it," Jacqueline Leo said. "She is three years old, and she can do little errands and she knows how to work the Xerox machine. I don't bring her in often, because of her schedule and mine, but I think she has a positive notion of work as being something that one simply does and there is clearly no sex role attached to it."

"I have always been very honest about my work with the kids," Pat Collins says. "For instance, I'll tell them, 'Today is going to be an ick day. I've got to work all day and all night, because I have to cover the Grammy awards. I'll have to change in the office, and you won't see me until tomorrow afternoon after school.' Like that. They always know what I am doing and what it is like."

The really big question, however, is, What kind of impact does the successful woman's career have on her children? Is it positive? Or negative?

There are negatives, and the women we interviewed were quick to point them out, but the positives seemed to far outweigh the negatives. This was to be expected. These women, without exception, are intensely child-oriented. They have the same desire and drive to be good mothers that they have to succeed in their careers. And they seem to be doing a good job of bringing up their children.

Felice Schwartz has what one might call proof of the pudding. Her three children are grown, and she thinks they are wonderful.

"I think the impact of my working was positive for them. My two boys would not have thought of marrying a woman who did not have a life of her own. They both married very high-achieving women.

"My daughter, Kathy, a photographer, is thirty-eight. She is married to a businessman and is pregnant for the first time.

Tony, a journalist, is thirty-four and married to an editor. My younger son, Jimmy, is just finishing his doctorate in math, and his wife is finishing hers in biochemistry.

"I was marvelously happy in what I was doing, and it was enriching for the children. I was constantly talking about combining family and work, and that became part of my children's thinking. And they all care profoundly in their own ways about making a difference for the better in this world.

"On the negative side, I think everyone around me—including myself—suffered from the fact that every minute of my life has always been programmed."

"I think the impact of my career has been mostly positive," Pat Collins said. "The kids have really got their feet on the ground.

"For instance, they have a good grasp of the downside of what appears to be the glamorous entertainment business, because they have heard me talk about how these people have made enormous sacrifices and about how most of them are not happy in their personal lives. Their exposure has shown them—unlike all these kids who are sixteen and want to be rock stars because they think it's such a wonderful life— that it is not all great. If you asked my daughter, Elizabeth, about it, my guess is that she would say, 'You know, you're only big for maybe six months and then your record company forgets about you.'

"They know all about the fleeting quality of instant fame. Elizabeth and I had a big discussion the other day on whether one would want to be Magellan or Madonna. It came up because she had to write a paper about explorers and Magellan was on the list. She concluded it would be better to be Magellan because it was quite unlikely that five hundred years from now anyone would be talking about Madonna, whereas someone would still be writing a paper on Magellan.

"They have also had to make certain decisions on their own. Part of me wishes that were not the case. I believe in letting children have a childhood. I guess there is a happy medium we must all try for between kids' getting enough exposure so they understand the reality of life around them and not having so much exposure that they don't have a real childhood.

"And there are nice little perks that were fun for them that they got because of my job. They were at the opening of Epcot and they were the first kids on the Dumbo ride in the Magic Kingdom and they were the ones that got to go to the Disney screening with Mommy and the first ones on the block to see *Back to the Future*. I think they had a feeling that they were getting a few extra little treats because of Mommy's otherwise demanding job.

"On the negative side, I think for Elizabeth—she's nine—that she felt there was a chunk of time that she and I were denied being together. I think she feels we are making up for it now, but every once in a while we will be talking and she will say, 'Remember when . . . ' and then she'll interrupt herself and say, 'Oh, yeah, you weren't there, Mom. You were in Los Angeles.' It is funny how they always remember these things.

"Elizabeth probably paid the greatest penalty for my working, because she was born two weeks late. It was a cesarean, and two weeks later I had to go right back to work, so we missed Mommy–Baby time together. And then three years later, when Andrew came along, he got a bit more attention, because he had some medical problems in the beginning. It was not that Elizabeth was jealous, just that she never got that feeling that she was getting all of my attention. I think that only in the last two years has she felt that she has gotten her share.

"I think the impact of my career on Juliet has been ninety-eight percent positive," Gillian Sorensen said. "Once I was having a particularly difficult time at work and I said, 'Oh, maybe I'll quit.' And then I added 'Wouldn't that be nice, Juliet? Then I would be home every day when you got here.'

And she said, 'Oh, no! Then you wouldn't have anything to do.'

"Juliet knows that there is family life and there is work life. Or to put it another way, there is love and there is work and both are important. She knows that a woman has responsibilities, has identity, has commitments and friends and colleagues. She also sees me in the domestic role and in the maternal role, when I am cooking and organizing her plans and helping with her homework and things like that, so she really has seen a multifaceted female role. I think all this is healthy."

Lynn Gilbert has a slightly different perspective. "They might feel a little cheated that I was not there a hundred percent of the time. If I stay home now, my daughter says, 'Oh, look at this! You're really being a mommy today. You're gonna cook and go to the cleaners'.' It's a joke, and we giggle a lot about it. She obviously has felt some of it missing.

"But I don't see anything negative. I have independent children, children who admire the work ethic, children with strong motivations and goals."

Lynn Redgrave says, "I think my working has had a positive effect on the children.

"The negative times have been when they really would have liked one to be at something that one couldn't be at, like a parents' day, and they want not to be the one who doesn't have a parent there, but we've missed very few of those type of events. I suppose the fact is that I do sometimes have to go away quite a lot.

"On the other hand, I think it's given them a sense of security, because we have concentrated very much, especially in the early years, on making them feel secure."

When I asked Joan Rivers about the impact of her career on Melissa, she said, "I think it's very mixed. I think a lot of positive things have happened. She has seen that a woman can go out and make her way in the world, that a woman

can be successful in 'a man's business,' that a woman can call
the shots.

"I think on the negative side that having a very successful
mother is very difficult. Having a high-pressure, high-powered mother is very difficult. Having a famous mother is very
difficult.

"I have tried to balance this by doing a lot of private things
with Melissa where we really shut the rest of the world out.
And I have made sure she knows she is important to me. It
is a question of delegating time intelligently and setting priorities intelligently. You don't go to every opening. You don't
go to every charity benefit. You stay home and you have
dinner with your child. You make sure you are at the Scout
meeting and the school play. You make sure you are there
to talk to them and find out what their problems are."

Joan is absolutely correct. It is not easy for a child to have
an extremely successful mother or a celebrity mother. A recent study of 355 children of successful parents found that
many of the children were underachievers or had other serious problems. "The parents set such perfect models," reported Dr. Anne Petersen, professor of human development
at Pennsylvania State University, "that the children saw the
goal of meeting or surpassing their parents' achievements as
just about impossible."

As I became more successful and better known, I worried
that Lisa might feel inadequate. I did not want her to feel
overwhelmed by my celebrity status. I wanted to find something where *she* could excel, something quite different from
what *I* was doing.

As it happened, Lisa found her own area of expertise. She
was taking riding lessons and turned out to be very good.
This was a field in which there was no possibility of her
achievement's being compared with mine. I had been bitten
by a horse when I was little and was—and still am—terrified
by the creatures, no matter how gentle. But Lisa was fearless.
She rode in shows and won ribbons for dressage and jump-

ing. She was really excellent. The riding gave her a sense of control and also a sense that she was competent in a field where her mother was an absolute flub.

"The impact of my working on Alexandra has been both good and bad," said Jacqueline Leo. "I think sometimes I bring home too much tension to give her the unqualified attention that she deserves. Pressure is pressure and it comes out in funny ways. I don't think of myself as having too short a fuse, but it is probably shortened in direct proportion to stress. So she has the downside of a career mother in that sense.

"At the same time she has the upside. Alexandra is growing up quite advantaged in that she has a lot of adult role models, not just the dictatorship of her parents. She moves in an extended family of friends and relatives. I think she is very privileged in the social sense."

A significant number of mothers said that their child's independence was the most noticeable impact of their working. Some women reported that their children were far more capable and self-reliant than they themselves had been as children. When Linda Tarry was asked about the impact of her career on her children, she said, "Well, let me take my older one. He is sixteen and has had a working mom since he was four years old.

"On the positive side, I think it has made him very independent. It has made him more resourceful, because there have been times when he has had to make decisions—not major decisions, but decisions—because I was not there to make them for him.

"On the negative side, there have been times when I came home from work and could have extended myself a bit more to hear what had gone on during his day. But I just didn't. I was bushed. I would come in, take off my shoes, take a hot shower and go to bed. I did not do it often, but often enough so that maybe someday I will look back and say, 'Boy, I should have shared more time with him.' "

"Both Jonathan and Jennifer are very independent kids," says Joyce Buchman. "And I think that's good. It is the positive effect of my working. I was not independent when I was young. I grew up in a very sheltered environment. I couldn't do anything. Until I was twenty-one years old, my father would call the dentist and say, 'I want my daughter to come in for a checkup.'

"It has had a positive impact on the children," Marilyn Moore reported. "They are extremely independent. They can do so much more than I could. They know so much more than I did even when I was ten years older than they are. They know how to cook. They know how to take care of themselves. They know how to grocery-shop. They know how to clean the house, wash clothes. When I was nineteen, I didn't even know how to wash a load of clothes."

"My working has made my son very independent and resourceful," says Karol Emmerich. "As far as negative impact, I don't think I'll know that for another ten years. To date, there is none. His teachers have uniformly said that he is one of the happiest, most affectionate, cheerful children they have ever had, which tells me he's not feeling neglected."

Karen Nussbaum is another who feels that her children are too young for her to gauge the impact of her work on them. "It's so hard to say when they are so young. It is just a fact of their lives—they go to school in the morning and I go to work and so does Daddy. They are happy, delightful children. I feel things are pretty good with them. I would know if they were having some problem. I would see it in their behavior, in their development. Right now I feel that they are doing well."

Linda Grant, who gave up her job to stay home with her baby, says, "I think about the impact of a mother's work on her children a lot. Sometimes when I am reading a wedding announcement in *The New York Times* and the woman getting married is rather accomplished and then I read that both parents worked, I think, 'Aha! No wonder. The mother worked.'

"It is a funny bias I have in favor of working mothers, which is in conflict with my feeling that you need to spend a lot of time with your children. I think when they are younger, it can be negative. I'm not sure anyone puts in the effort that a mother does. But I think that when the children are older, it is probably a better example for them to see both parents go to work rather than seeing one parent stay home and the other go to work."

So there you are. We are talking about role models again. These children have had role models, both male and female, who have worked outside the home. And they will be the role models of tomorrow.

Are these children significantly different from their peers who have grown up with stay-home mothers? This is an impossible question to answer at this time. Yale psychologist Edward Zigler's answer to the effects of day care applies here as well. "We are not going to know until they grow up and raise children of their own."

There are indications that the children of this group of successful women may be more independent and self-reliant than the children of stay-home mothers, but it is impossible to say how much more, just as it is impossible to say whether the children of other working mothers are as independent or more independent or less independent than these relatively privileged children.

It also may be that these children have had richer lives, met more people, been exposed to more experiences and ideas than the children of stay-home mothers, but again, this is an undocumented generalization. And there is no way of telling how significant this exposure to people, ideas and experiences will prove to be.

What does seem evident is that none of these children seem

to have suffered from the lifestyles imposed by their mothers' careers.

Will these women's daughters follow in their mothers' footsteps? Again, it is too early to tell. My guess is that their very independent daughters will do whatever seems right for them.

Jennifer Buchman, for instance, the daughter of investment counselor Joyce Buchman, is not convinced that she wants a career, despite her mother's obvious relish in her work.

"Jennifer turned to me a couple of years ago," Joyce said, "and asked, 'Will you be very disappointed if I am only a wife and mother? I may not want a career.'

"And I said, 'Jennifer, there is nothing more important than being a good wife and mother, but I hope that you will work, because you can do both.'

"She is a history major at Vassar, and she worked last summer in an antiques shop on Madison Avenue. She has wonderful taste and she loves selling antiques. I am sure she will work."

Time will tell. Time will tell its story for Jennifer as well as the other daughters and sons of this group of women. What can be said here and now is that their mothers love them and are proud of them. Not one woman voiced disappointment in her child or her child's development.

PART FIVE

CAREER

TWENTY-THREE

TALK ABOUT temptation. Talk about seduction. Talk about work! The majority of the women we interviewed talked about their work with a passion that had not been sparked by their marriages or even their children. They love their families, but they are enamored of their work. They feel that it has widened their horizons, given them a sense of accomplishment, expanded their potential, given them their identity, freed them to be their best. In *Point Counter Point,* Aldous Huxley wrote, "If they stopped working, they'd realize they simply weren't there at all, most of them. Just holes in the air, that's all." Many of these women seemed to feel that they had indeed been "holes in the air" until they had been created by their work. Some referred to their careers as their salvation.

"My work has been a salvation. It has been an extraordinary experience, a challenge, an avenue for growth and creativity."
—GILLIAN SORENSEN

"I love my work more than I love anything else. My work is who I am." —JONI EVANS

"If I had not worked, I don't think I would have been happy. I needed to do what I did." —FELICE SCHWARTZ

"My work is essential for me to survive. Without my work, without being able to write, without having my own identity, I would just wither away and die. I couldn't live without it. It is as essential to me as having a relationship with a man and having my child." —SALLY QUINN

"My work has been wonderful for me. It was where I got all the warm fuzzies that I didn't get in my personal life." —IDA ROBERTS, Vice President of Corporate Communications, SE Bank Corporation.

"It made me develop as a person, made me grow. My work has expanded my horizons." —SHEILA KURTZ, a certified hand-writing analyst and president of her own company, A New Slant.

"I don't know what I would do without my work. I'll always work—as long as I can. I love it." —JOYCE BUCHMAN

"I found a great salvation through acting. It did a fantastic amount for me—making the person that I really am feel free to just be that." —LYNN REDGRAVE

These women are not isolated examples. What they are talking about is the psychic income they get from their work—the sense of identity, of competence, of creativity, of success. According to a *New York Times* survey of more than 1,300 people, women find work just as satisfying as marriage and children.

And there are other benefits. Successful women have a 29 percent higher life expectancy than other women, according to the Metropolitan Life Insurance Company. Success is a form of winning. And "winning," say Dr. Ernest Vander-weghe and Dr. Laurence Morehouse of the Human Performance Laboratories at UCLA, "has a profound positive effect on a person's self-esteem and well-being."

Women may even enjoy success more than men. "More and more successful people are becoming troubled, conflicted or emotionally damaged by their work and career climb," says Dr. Douglas LaBier, a Washington, D.C., psychoanalyst who has studied the effects of success. "It is the lucky ones who have developed a life of balance in keeping with their full values."

I suspect there is a disproportionate number of women among these "lucky ones," and that women derive more satisfaction than conflict or emotional damage from success, simply because their lives are fuller, are more balanced. On the basis of the women we spoke with, most successful women devote more time and thought and energy to their marriage and their children than successful men do. They are used to keeping several balls in the air at one time. And even though the greatest challenge and excitement may come from their work, they are still deeply involved in the other aspects of their lives.

Almost every woman spoke of the confidence she had gained from her work. They spoke of meeting hurdles, conquering them and gaining courage to face even higher hurdles.

"I am a more interesting person than I would be if I didn't work," says Mary Cunningham. "And more confident. Work has challenged me, and I believe challenges make you a more confident person, because you are constantly testing your ability to rise to the occasion. The tougher the challenges and the more you are able to rise above them, the more confident you become. Ultimately you feel that you can handle whatever is going to be put in your path."

"I am more independent," says Jane Kennedy. "It has made me rely on my own instincts. I am stronger. I've learned to stand up for myself and for what I believe because of my work. I have learned that I have a lot of creativity. I believe in myself.

"I've grown up in my work," Joni Evans says. "Working

hard and working the way I do has turned me into who I am. I have always been the typical workaholic. The fear of failure—never the fear of success—has driven me. Every new challenge, I think, 'Oh, I'm not going to be able to do it.' But with each success comes more confidence. And more sense of adventure. And more risk-taking. Success has made me better at what I do, because I am free to take bigger gambles."

Lois Wyse told me, "As I became more successful, I became more confident, less concerned about what other people thought of me, more concerned with satisfying the people who are close to me and far less concerned with satisfying the general public."

"My work has made me grow tremendously," says Marilyn Moore. "When I was a child, I was so shy I never even made a phone call. I had my sister do it for me. I have a lot of confidence now that I didn't have before. And I understand people better."

Gillian Sorensen says, "It has prompted me to be braver and bolder than I ever thought I could be, to take on new initiatives and responsibilities, to speak up and speak out, to take a public role, to lead and manage an office.

"I have had an opportunity to serve the city I love and at the same time work with that most extraordinary and diverse community, the diplomatic corps from 159 countries. There are moments when I know that something I have been able to resolve has made a difference, so I am paid both financially and psychically."

Every career has its drawbacks, and I was surprised that more women did not mention them. Only three women brought up negative aspects of their success. It was clear that the pluses far outweighed the minuses. The negatives that were mentioned all had to do with some aspect of the quality of life.

Pat Collins regretted that she had become less trusting and more cynical. "I am not as trusting and open-minded about business as I was when I started," she reported, "when I felt that if you built contacts and friendships, they would never be violated. I have been burned enough times to realize you have to be much more cautious about what you tell people and with whom you decide to cast your lot in business.

"I *am* more commercially minded. I look at an idea and I think, 'I like this, but I don't think anybody is going to go for it.' Whereas fifteen years ago, I'd be saying, 'God, this is great! We gotta get somebody to do this!' Experience has taught me that they probably aren't going to do it, and we should go to the next thing. So I am a little less trusting and a little more cynical."

Jacqueline Leo worries about the erosion of courtesy in her life. "I am constantly trying to make sure I don't lose all my good manners," she says. "Part of it is being sharp. I don't mean being nasty, but being terse. You are trying to get as much packed into every minute as possible. The little things that are so wonderful—remembering people's birthday, writing the thank-you notes and finding the time for all that quality-of-life stuff—tends to go out the window."

Heloise had mild complaints about the downside of celebrity. "The negative side is when you don't want to be recognized," she said. "When you want to go to the store and buy toilet paper when it's on sale and people follow you up and down the aisles looking to see what's in your cart. My husband won't go to the store with me anymore."

The emphasis with practically every woman was on growth, challenge, stimulation, self-discovery, increased competence and knowledge, even salvation.

"My work has changed me," Lynn Redgrave says. "I don't know whether it has to do with success or whether I found a great salvation through acting.

"I found that turning into other people liberated me. I did not particularly like myself when I began acting. I felt I was very unattractive. Then I discovered that when I was on stage, I could believe—and make other people believe—that I was beautiful. I could make people believe that I was much older or much younger. I could make people laugh. I could make people cry. I found that I could be anything that I wanted to be on the stage. And I could believe in that life on the stage for the duration of the performance or, if it was a film, for the duration of the filming.

"Being reasonably bright, it eventually occurred to me that if I could do that through being other people, why couldn't I somehow find myself and have the same sort of enjoyment in myself.

"I think that acting did a fantastic amount for me as far as making the person that I really am feel free to just be that."

"I have learned to handle myself fairly well in public and to think on my feet," said Linda Tarry. "At one point I hosted a television talk show on Channel Two in New York for almost two years. It prepared me for where I am now, and it was a very accidental process. I just happened to answer an ad and auditioned against a thousand women and got the slot.

"It was a talk show. There was no script. Anyone could throw a provocative question at you and you had to be prepared, because there you were—right on television.

"It prepared me for the business world, where you have the same type of situation. And it has helped me to walk into a room as a woman—and I may add, as a black woman—in this world of high tech, which is predominantly a white male environment, and deal with those looks you get for a split second and then getting down to business and doing what I am there for."

"My career tests my energy, my integrity, my inventiveness. It has expanded me enormously intellectually," said Carole Sinclair, adding that her success has resulted in her becoming kinder, more generous and more understanding. "I've become more generous with myself and my time," Carole said, "because I appreciate people who are generous with me. I find myself for the first time acting as a role model for people, a mentor."

Sally Quinn felt the same way. "Having written a successful novel," she says, "I feel a lot better about myself; therefore I feel better about other people. I think that when you are happy with yourself, then you are more generous about other people. So being successful has changed me that way."

"My work has helped me understand people better," Sheila Kurtz, a handwriting analyst, says. "I am more patient. I now look to the left and right more instead of just having tunnel vision. I have developed a sense of humor. It made me develop as a person."

"I think I am a much nicer person because of my work," said Karen Nussbaum. "As I have become successful—or because I've gotten older—I am a more patient person. I have much more perspective. I am more generous toward other people and situations."

For some women, work is a comforter. Earlier in this book I made the point that in today's world, every woman should be able to support herself and her children. Just in case. But work can be more than a fail-safe, more than a bulwark against need. Women testified that their work had helped them find and express themselves, that it had helped them "rock along" when other parts of their lives were painful or disappointing.

Ida Roberts, vice president of corporate communications, SE Bank Corporation, said, "If I had not worked while I was married, I would have ended up one of these displaced-homemaker, dominated types, and that would have been a tragedy. My work was a real confidence-builder for me. If you are in a bad marriage, a career helps. It gives you some diversion. It makes it a little easier to rock along."

Lois Wyse came up with another, very special, perspective on the benefits of a career. "When your children grow up and their day-to-day dependency on you lessens, it is a very great comfort not to have a dependency on them. The best thing about having worked is that I don't have a parasitic need for my children. I can let them go off and live their own lives and see them when I see them and not wonder why my daughter doesn't call me every day."

Few of these women fit the pattern of the driven career woman. They love their work, but with only two or three exceptions, their work is not the whole of their lives. It is a seductive and exciting part of their lives, but most of them would agree with actress Sissy Spacek who said, "You know, your career is just your career. Your life is your *life!*"

And these women all feel they have wonderful lives.

TWENTY-FOUR

HAPPINESS SEEMS to be one of the perks of success. Without exception, each and every one of the women I interviewed seemed to relish her life. It was not that their lives were that fictional bed of roses. All of them had had to cope with disappointment, personal tragedies and professional setbacks, but by and large these women radiated a solid satisfaction with life.

I also came to realize how very individual a state happiness is. I was not tempted to change places with any one of these women. I had no hankering to be a diplomat or an actress or a labor activist or a corporate wheel. I think my own life is pretty wonderful, but I do not believe that many other women would really want to walk in my shoes.

Most people seem to have a picture of me as a pampered celebrity, chauffeured from television studio to lecture platform to business appointment in a stretch limousine, sampling the famous restaurants and glittering night life on both coasts and spending my weekends in an exquisitely restored farmhouse set among manicured acres. Not true. Not true at all.

Oh, there is a germ of truth in it. I do rush from television studio to lecture platform or to another television studio or out on location with a television crew for a news shoot. But not in a limo. I hail a cab or drive myself or go in the van with the crew. When I have an out-of-town speaking engagement, it is true I am met at the airport by a limousine, but the rest of the time my transportation is much less glamorous.

As for those fancy restaurants and the glittering night life on both coasts, forget it. When I'm in Los Angeles, I fight jet lag by staying on New York time as much as I can. That means that I am in bed by nine (midnight, New York time) unless I am scheduled to give an evening lecture or do a late interview for KNX radio. And when I am at home, I cook dinner. Milt and I rarely go out at night. When we do, it is an occasion—the theater or the ballet or a night baseball game.

We do spend almost all our weekends at our farm. And yes, the house was restored. By loving hands. Mine and Milt's. We ripped up layers of linoleum to get down to the original wide-board floors, broke through walls to make rooms larger, sanded, wallpapered, painted. You name it, we did it. Our acres are hardly what you would call landscaped, let alone manicured. We do keep the garden weeded. We mow the grass around the house and between the trees in the orchard we planted. But a showplace it's not. And except for the snowplowing, Milt and I do all the work. And love it.

What are my days really like? Busy is the common denominator. No two days are alike, but there is a certain pattern to them, depending on whether I am at home or traveling. The details change, but the structure remains. Let me sketch two days in my life and you will see what I mean.

AT HOME

6:30 a.m.: I get up. I take out the curlers that I invented. The great thing about them is that they allow me to sleep, and when I comb out my hair, it looks as if I have used hot rollers. I mean to patent these curlers one day when I have a minute.

I shower and head for the scale. I weigh myself every single morning before breakfast, when I am lightest. I do not let myself gain more than one pound, and when I gain that pound, I make immediate corrections in my diet.

I put on a robe and head for the kitchen. I squeeze the orange juice, and Milt makes the coffee. I set the table and make toast. Milt picks up the morning paper at the door, and we sit down to breakfast. We read and talk, mostly about what is in the newspaper, since neither of us really has it together yet.

I clear the table, put the dishes in the sink and get dressed.

8:00 a.m.: Milt leaves for his office. I head for my home office, just around the corner from the kitchen. I work on my column or the mail for an hour before my staff arrives. My staff consists of two or three (it varies) college women and young mothers who want to work part time. They answer the telephone and type and cope with the million and one details that my television, lecture and writing commitments involve. They also keep my research files up to date. Three walls of my office are lined with filing cabinets that contain background research. I am always adding to these files, which are probably my most valuable working asset.

10:00 a.m.: I take the elevator down from our 30th-floor apartment and walk across to the garage for my car. I head for NBC Radio, in midtown Manhattan.

10:45 a.m.: I walk into the NBC studio. I am going to tape five radio spots today. I give the producer the five scripts I have prepared. He edits a couple of the scripts, shortening them. I have to admit that he is right. The taping goes well. We are through at noon.

Noon: The producer and director hurry off—one to a meeting, the other to a business lunch.

I rarely schedule business lunches—no more than five or six times a year. I find they take too much time. I can get more done in less time in someone's office than over the luncheon table. In an office, the executive usually has another appointment scheduled after mine, so we get right down to business. When I go out to lunch, I have found that people usually wait until coffee is served to start talking business.

Today I am due at WABC-TV at one o'clock. I go to the ladies' room and freshen my makeup, then take the elevator down to the garage to get my car and drive uptown to ABC.

1:00 p.m.: The producer, the executive producer and I discuss the news shoot that is scheduled for this afternoon. The producer has set up the interview and obtained permission to film. Now we go over the approach. I will be interviewing Dr. Brian L. G. Morgan, professor at the Institute for Human Nutrition at the College of Physicians and Surgeons. Dr. Morgan has done some interesting research indicating that—in rats, at least—breast milk seems to have an effect on intelligence.

2:00 p.m.: The cameraman, the producer and I set up in Dr. Morgan's office. He is a little uncomfortable in front of the camera at first, but as he starts talking about his work he relaxes. I think the interview has gone well. Ilene Rosen, the producer, agrees.

3:30 p.m.: Back at ABC. Ilene and I discuss another segment in this series that we plan to shoot in the near future. I pick up my car and stop off at my mother's apartment on the way home for a quick hello and a kiss.

On days when I do not have a news shoot or a future-projects meeting at ABC, I do those things that I can't delegate—like going to the dentist, getting my hair cut, shopping for something spectacular to wear on an evening talk show: that kind of thing.

4:15 p.m.: Back home again. I check my messages and then I call the butcher. Milt and I do most of our food shopping together on weekends, but I tend not to buy meat until I need it. Today I have decided to make osso buco for dinner, so I call the butcher and order two veal shanks and ask him to cut them into two-inch lengths.

5:15 p.m.: I put the veal shanks in the oven to simmer in their sauce for an hour and a half. I clean up the kitchen and set the table and go back to my office, where I return West Coast telephone calls, make notes for a future column and review my schedule for tomorrow, when I am booked to speak before the Kansas Bar Association, which is meeting in Wichita.

6:00 p.m.: Milt arrives home. We talk for a while, then he watches the local news on TV while I finish getting dinner.

7:00 p.m.: We eat dinner. Afterwards, Milt helps me with the dishes. (If he feels like being pampered, he'll say, "I'll do my half later." But he never does.)

8:00 p.m.: We couch-potato it in front of the TV right through the eleven o'clock news.

Midnight: Milt goes off to bed and I go to my office to work on my book.

1:45 a.m.: I'm finally off to bed. And I have to catch a seven o'clock flight tomorrow for Kansas!

IN LOS ANGELES

I usually spend one day in Los Angeles every couple of weeks doing television shows, ranging from talk shows to appearances on *Mama's Family* or *Moonlighting* to spots on news shows. I also spend a day or two a week, sometimes three days, out of town speaking before different groups. Most of the time I can do this without spending the night, although I may not get home until well after midnight. But having breakfast with Milt means more to me than a full night's sleep.

I have learned to make strange beds feel almost like my own. I always pack my own pillow and a soft wool bed pad just like the ones on my bed at home. And speaking of packing, I always have two suitcases packed and ready to go. Makeup, curlers, clothes, pillow, bed pad—everything I need for an overnight stay. I make so many fast turnarounds that this saves time and energy. It also means that I can pick up and go at a moment's notice.

The night before I leave for Los Angeles, I fill the electric coffee maker and squeeze the orange juice, so all I have to do in the morning is switch on the coffee maker and pop a slice of bread in the toaster. While I am waiting for the coffee, I call the taxi company to remind them that I have ordered a cab for five forty-five. I pad around the house, get washed and dressed and leave while Milt is still sleeping.

To me, planes are offices in the sky. I have a number of sturdy canvas tote bags that have wheels on the bottom so you really don't have to tote them. You can just drag them after you. I fill a bag with all the mail on my desk and reading matter—newspapers, psychological journals, magazines—when I go on a trip.

I read my mail and scribble notes on each letter. Sometime during the day I will try to find a few minutes to dictate replies over the telephone to one of the women in my office, so they will be ready for my signature when I get home. I read through everything and tear out articles that interest me for my files. The rest of the magazines and papers are jettisoned. I never throw away letters. So many people write me about very personal matters that I keep the letters until I get home. The ones that are not filed are incinerated.

When I finish, I pull out a notebook and get to work on

my next column or a radio script or my book. At least half of this book was written in the air between New York and Los Angeles.

11:30 a.m.: The plane lands in Los Angeles. I grab my suitcase from the baggage carousel and run for the car-rental counter. I have a business appointment on Sunset Boulevard at noon and drive directly there.

12:30 p.m.: I am starving. My stomach is on New York time, where it is half past three. I pick up my car and head for the Beverly Hills Hotel. The minute I'm in my room, I call room service for a glass of milk and a chicken sandwich. I shower and change.

2:00 p.m.: I drive to KNX Radio, where I am scheduled to tape a spot on the psychology behind the news. The subject is a wave of shootings on the Los Angeles freeways. I have prepared a rough script. The producer goes over it and suggests some changes. I make a couple of telephone calls to check if there have been any new developments. We go over the script again and then move to the studio to get it on tape.

4:00 p.m.: I drive to Norman Brokaw's office in Beverly Hills. Norman is my agent. We discuss a possible appearance on a new sitcom.

6:00 p.m.: Back at the hotel. It is nine o'clock New York time. The way I fight jet lag is to stay on New York time as much as possible when I am away from home. I call room service and ask for an omelet and a salad. While I am waiting for my supper to arrive, I call Milt. I call him every night I'm away from home. I tell him what's gone on in my day, that I'm excited at the possibility of the new sitcom, but I'm not sure how it will work out. He tells me Lisa called and that the new astronomy book he ordered came and he is reading it.

My supper arrives. The hotel maid turns down my bed. When she leaves, I spread my woolen pad over the bottom sheet and substitute my down pillow for the hotel pillow.

9:00 p.m.: I push the serving table out into the corridor, call the desk and ask for a wake-up call at four tomorrow morning, when it will be seven o'clock in New York.

4:00 a.m.: The telephone rings. "Good morning. This is your wake-up call." I get out of bed and do a few exercises—stretches and bends and easy sit-ups. I shower, and while the rest of Los Angeles is sleeping, I work on my book.

6:00 a.m.: I order breakfast and the newspapers. When I finish, I put on my makeup and get dressed. Then I go over my notes. I am scheduled to address a group of top executives in the electronics field at a seven-thirty breakfast meeting at the Century Plaza on how to keep research-and-development staffs motivated.

8:45 a.m.: The meeting went well. There was a very good question-and-answer period afterwards. They tell me they want to schedule a similar meeting for a larger group seven or eight months from now. This is always flattering. I get my car and head for the airport, where I drop off the car and load up my tote bag with magazines and papers from the newsstand.

10:00 a.m.: The plane taxis down the runway. Next stop New York.

There you are. Two days crammed full of work and travel and love. Even though I miss being with Milt when I'm away, the telephone is a wonderful bridge between us. My monthly bills are horrendous, but the benefits are even greater. We do not have a chance to grow apart, to get used to being without each other. I make sure that Milt always knows what is going on in my life. I never hand him any surprises like "Oh, did I tell you, I'm leaving for Hong Kong tomorrow?" When I go on a major—or minor—trip, he knows about it almost as soon as I do. And it works the other way. I always know what his days are like, the problems he faces, the satisfactions he has.

I dwell on this because I have seen too many women take their marriages and families for granted after a while. If you want to have it all—or most of it—you can't take anything for granted. Marriages, just like careers, need constant nurturing. And I don't think of this nurturing as a task, but as a pleasure, a joy. When you come right down to it, the secret of having it all is loving it all.

TWENTY-FIVE

How RELEVANT is it to the young woman who has not yet achieved career success to learn how successful women cope with career, husband and children? Extremely relevant, I believe. Most of the women who shared their experiences in this book were pioneers. They had few role models. They juggled the various aspects of their lives as best they could and managed to keep everything moving forward—even if not always at an even rate. Learning from experience is great, but it can be painful. Learning from someone else's experience is always easier. Just knowing how other women have coped with the hundreds of minor and major crises that arise when the demands of children, husband and career collide can be reassuring as well as instructive.

CAREER

None of the women in this book was born successful. Each one of them worked for her success. None of them achieved success overnight. Some made false starts. Julie Eisenhower at one point thought she wanted to teach. Others had career setbacks that were emotionally wrenching. Mary Cunningham got caught in the middle of corporate infighting at Bendix. Still others, like Jeane Kirkpatrick and Joyce Buchman, stayed home for several years while their children were young.

"I understand all that," a college senior told me at a career seminar. "I'm willing to work hard. I think I'm strong enough to cope with setbacks. But how do you become a success when you haven't the foggiest idea of what you can do—or even what you want to do? All I know," she said, "is that I want to be a success. I want to be tops at something."

"Half the successful people in the world," I told her, "didn't know what they wanted to do either. All they knew was that, like you, they wanted to do something and do it very well. They wanted to achieve. The main thing is to get out and do *something*. Everything you do helps you know yourself and what you want to do and can do better."

Some people know from age eight or twelve or twenty-one that they are going to be doctors or pianists or actresses or designers or whatever. And they progress in a straight line toward that goal.

Other people zigzag through life for a while until they find their direction. I think my daughter, Lisa, might have been a zigzagger if I had not given her a motherly nudge. She had very vague ideas about her future when she was at Princeton. Once she told me, "I think I'm going to be a writer after I graduate." "Fine," I said. "I'd love to see what you have been writing lately."

Lisa hemmed and hawed and then admitted that she really had not written anything that semester. Perhaps writing was

not what she really wanted to do. After that, she had brief
enthusiasms for one career or another, but nothing really
grabbed her.

One weekend when I drove down to visit her, she was
fretting about not having a direction for her future. "Let's
look over your courses," I suggested, "and see if there are
any clues there." She had taken more science courses than I
had realized—and done very well in them. I did not want to
say anything like "I think you ought to go to medical school.
You've done so well in biology and chemistry." All that that
would produce would be an "Oh, Mother!" I did point out,
however, that she needed only two more science courses to
qualify for medical school. "You don't have to go," I said,
"but the door would be open for you if you decided to." That
made sense to her. A year later she was accepted at Tulane
University Medical School.

Lisa probably would have gone into medicine anyway.
Everything seemed to point in that direction, but without
that little nudge, it might have taken her longer to realize
that this was what she really wanted.

One of Lisa's friends did a lot of zigzagging. Phyllis first
worked as a research assistant on a newsmagazine. She left
that job after two years to work as a trainee in the time-buying
department of an advertising agency. After a couple of promotions, she took a job in the advertising department of a
Fifth Avenue department store. Today, at thirty-two, she is
the advertising director of a major cosmetics company.

Looking back, everything Phyllis did was a kind of ap-
prenticeship for her present position, even though she had
no master plan or even a sense of destination. When I asked
her what she saw in her future, she laughed. "Everything
and anything," she said. "Maybe I'll have my own agency one
day."

Phyllis and Lisa are a lot alike—successful professionals,
happily married wives and mothers. But Lisa will probably
be an ophthalmologist all her working life, while Phyllis will

probably move on in directions she may not even have considered yet until she finds the challenge that will hold her interest.

There is more to success, however, than knowing what you want to do and be and working hard to get there. Just recently I was in the ladies' room at ABC-TV, freshening up my makeup. Two women were sharing the mirror with me.

"I'm so depressed," one said. "All my friends are so successful and I'm nowhere. Just nowhere! I'm never going to make it. When I think of how well everyone else has done, what successes they are, I get so depressed. I just don't seem able to get anywhere, no matter how hard I try. I'm so far behind, I'll never catch up."

I was torn between wanting to give her a hug and a lecture. She could not have been more than twenty-one or twenty-two. The idea of feeling such a dismal failure at her age was almost funny. Funny and tragic. Tragic, because of her conviction that she could never succeed, which could be a self-fulfilling prophecy.

All successful people have something in common. Every successful person whom I have interviewed has said that he or she had always felt special. I always felt special as far back as I can remember. I had no idea when I was in grade school that I would be a celebrity, but I just knew I was special.

Recent studies show that there is a definite connection between this belief that one is special and success. "Research on the links between achievement, motivation and self-image," says psychologist Hazel Markus of the University of Michigan, "suggests that possible selves—future selves—are part of one's present self-image and are the keys to success or failure." A possible self, she says, "might include a successful self, a rich self and a loved self." If you see these as possible selves for you, it is quite likely that you will achieve them. By the same token, if you see yourself as a special person, you will turn out to be a special person.

My advice: If you are unsure of your career direction, even after doing a Goal Analysis (see Chapter Five), don't fret. Go out and get a job. Preferably a job that interests you. But almost any job is better than none. Once you have mastered that job, look around for the next step. Everything you do will help you know more about what you want.

Don't be afraid of making mistakes. One mistake or a half-dozen will not ruin your career as long as you learn from each mistake.

Believe in yourself. If you do, others will.

MARRIAGE

Most of the women in this book married and started their families while they were on the way up. Most, not all. And not all the marriages worked out. The second marriages seemed to be more successful, probably because the women knew more about themselves.

There is no doubt that marriage complicates life for the working woman. She may have to cope with a husband who does not want her to work or who earns less than she does or in some way feels diminished by her working. And she has to find ways to run the household as well as to devote the necessary time and energy and imagination to her career.

Today's young women are going to have it better than their predecessors. Life is going to be easier for them on the home front in at least one way. Surveys show that there is significantly more equal sharing of household chores in dual-career families under age thirty. This is as it should be, but it has taken a long time to become a matter of course. Not that every young husband will pull his fair weight around the house, but more and more of them are doing so. And surveys of teen-agers show that roughly 60 percent of them believe that husbands should share equally in everything from changing diapers to vacuuming. This sharing of domestic chores and child care can ease a working woman's life, give her an occasional moment to herself, dissipate much of the stress.

When women are asked to pinpoint the happiest times of their marriage, most say that the early years were the best. There is something special about those early years. The whole world lies ahead for the two of you. I always tell people that true love is when you are as concerned about the other person as you are about yourself. This mutual concern is often most powerful in the early years of marriage, when it is reinforced by sexual and emotional euphoria. You discover that marriage enables you to do more and be more than you ever thought possible.

Milt and I had some very rough times when we first got married. We had no money. We had to live with my folks. When we finally could afford a place of our own, it was a borderline slum. But, you know, it was wonderful! We were so happy! And even when things were at their rockiest, we knew it wasn't going to be forever. We *knew* we weren't going to live in that miserable walk-up all our lives.

And when I won *The Sixty-four Thousand Dollar Question* and we moved, it was the happiest move we ever made. We walked around our new apartment—one bedroom with an alcove for the baby, a tiny kitchen and just room for a table for two in the foyer—and thought it was just perfect.

I wouldn't want anyone to miss the happiness that we enjoyed in those years on the way up. We occasionally reminisce about them, and it always makes us feel even closer and more in love than ever.

My advice: Don't put off marriage for your career. Some women postpone marriage until they are established in their careers, but my advice would be to marry if you have found a man you love. As I said, the two of you can do more than either one of you alone. Don't rush into marriage for the sake of being married, of course, but if you meet the right man, marry him.

Conversely, if you feel marriage is not for you, don't let

peer pressure or family pressure force you into it. Years and
years ago, someone wrote a book called *Live Alone and Like
It*. I would not like it, but it is a choice some women make
and like.

CHILDREN

There is never a good time to have a child, never a perfect
time. Although some women we interviewed postponed starting their family until they were established in their careers,
most took that leap of faith into motherhood fairly early in
marriage. And not one, as far as I can tell, regretted it.

In most cases, the younger you are when you have your
children, the easier it is all around. I am glad I had Lisa in
my twenties and not in my late thirties or early forties. I am
not sure how patient a mother I would be today to a ram-
bunctious teen-ager. Being a grandparent suits me just fine.
It is quite clear to me that Lisa handles her children far more
easily than I do when Milt and I have them for a few days.

There is also something to be said for having your children
on your way up. They get a chance to share in the exhilaration
of achieving. They are also conscious of the setbacks, the
occasional failures and the trade-offs that must be made.
They get a healthy dose of reality and are not as likely to see
their parents as supermen and superwomen whom they will
never be able to equal or surpass.

Young women today will probably find it easier to juggle
job and children than it was for earlier generations of women.
Young husbands are more willing to assume their share of
responsibility for child care. And many young women are
beginning to see child care as a respected profession, rather
than a dead-end job. "Nanny" schools are being set up to
train women to care for young children. Unfortunately, the
salaries these professionally trained women can command
are too high for most young families to afford.

The need for more and better child care is underlined by

1987 Labor Department figures showing that more than half the women who have children under six years old work outside the home. While an increasing number of companies are providing day care for employees' children, the rate of increase is discouragingly slow. One survey shows that out of 46,000 middle- to large-size companies in this country, only 3,300 provide any kind of child-care help. It is clear that the corporate consciousness still needs raising. And so does government consciousness.

Women have the means to change this and change it rapidly. If every mother in this country, if every woman in this country wrote her congressman or congresswoman and senator, on both state and national levels, that her vote was going to the lawmakers who supported legislation providing care for the children of working mothers, we would see results instead of talk. It is time that women swung into action.

My advice: If you want a child, go ahead, unless there are circumstances that would make this an unwise or even foolish decision. Only you can be the judge. But later may be too late.

If, however, you do not want a child, do not let yourself be coerced into having one. If you are of two minds about whether or not to have a child, wait until you are absolutely sure. Put yourself first. Think long and hard. Read what the women whom we interviewed for this book have to say about children. And then make your decision.

When it comes to relevance, the life experiences of the successful women in these pages have a great deal of relevance for younger women. Life is a matter of choices. Examining the choices other women have made in similar situations—and their consequences—allows you to adopt, adapt or reject. I have always been grateful for the example of my mother, one of the very few women of her generation to combine a professional career with marriage and children. And my daughter has benefited from my example. She has made different choices in some areas, but when it came to the major choices, Lisa did not hesitate. She chose a career. She chose marriage and children. She knew what it would be like. But she also knew that she could handle it. She knew that her grandmother had. She knew that I had. Her life is very hard right now, with three small children and a busy practice, but it is a happy and rewarding life. And that is my wish for every woman.

TWENTY-SIX

So WE come back to the question: can a woman have it all? This is a question that should really not be asked. It seems to imply that a woman is lacking if she does not achieve this "all." We do not expect men to take the major responsibility for raising their children and maintaining a home and marriage as well as succeeding in their chosen field. Why should we expect it of women? But the answer to the question is— yes, if that is what a woman wants; but it is not easy. A third of the successful women we interviewed have been divorced at least once. Some never married. Some never remarried. Some postponed their careers to have children. Some postponed their children to have careers. Some never had children.

The women who were juggling marriage and children and career were realistic about what their lives entailed. As Barbara Hendricks said, "When people want to have it all, they want it to run like honey. Life is not like that." It truly is not. Having it all involves accepting trade-offs and understanding that not all aspects of your life are going to be satisfactory at any given moment. It involves making choices.

It was obvious in the course of our interviews that these successful women—whether or not they were married or had children—were happy. Whatever their lives were like, they had chosen them. They felt free to pursue their goals. This may be the essence of happiness.

INDEX